Language Smarts™ Series

📖 Level B 📖 Level C 📖 Level D 📖 Level E

Written by
Judy Wilson Goddard
Kathy Erickson

Graphic Design by
Danielle West
Scott Slyter

Edited by
Patricia Gray

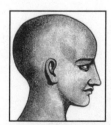

© 2011, 2006
THE CRITICAL THINKING CO.™
(Bright Minds™)
www.CriticalThinking.com
Phone: 800-458-4849 • Fax: 831-393-3277
P.O. Box 1610 • Seaside • CA 93955-1610
ISBN 978-0-89455-888-7

ABOUT THE AUTHORS

JUDY WILSON GODDARD has worn many hats; she served as a teacher and administrator in both private and public school settings, working with pre-school through college level students. Throughout her diverse career, she always maintained that critical thinking was important for all levels. Since her retirement, she has continued to promote critical thinking skills by writing books for children. She is the author of many books that apply critical thinking skills to a wide range of academic disciplines. She holds three degrees in education from Georgia State University: Bachelor, Master, and Specialist.

KATHY ERICKSON is a longtime newspaper editor whose first love was English. It was her favorite subject in school, and her major in college. She used that love of the language in writing and editing news stories. Between newspaper assignments, Erickson also worked as the media director for the Oregon PTA, and worked closely with parents, teachers, and volunteers in supporting and enhancing educational opportunities for children. This award-winning writer used her background in journalism and education to craft activities in this book to engage the young readers and challenge them to think critically.

TABLE OF CONTENTS

TABLE OF CONTENTS (cont.)

STANDARDS

ABOUT THIS BOOK

Language Smarts Level C will improve your students' reading, writing, spelling, punctuation, grammar, and thinking skills. The activities in this book deal with real-world objects and situations that students can relate to. Students will love the humor and challenge of the activities that teach and develop second-grade language arts concepts.

Thinking Skills

The activities require students to analyze a variety of diagrams and apply problem-solving skills. Targeted thinking skills include convergent and divergent thinking as well as inductive and deductive reasoning. Students will learn to recognize, analyze, and synthesize information.

Role of the Student and Teacher/Parent

Although the activities are fun and tantalizing, they are also challenging. To avoid student frustration and to get the most out of these activities, please be ready to support students with clues—not answers—when they need help. Whenever possible, ask the students to explain their answers and then follow up their answers with more questions that challenge their understanding. Finally, remember to praise students for their efforts and remind them how smart they are to solve these challenging activities. If students grow tired or frustrated, encourage them to finish the problem, but do not force them. Problem-solving should be stimulating and engaging, not a chore.

Classroom Application

The activities can serve as your second-grade language arts core curriculum or as a supplemental resource. The language arts thinking skills covered in this book are very effective preparation for standardized tests.

Long Vowels

A **long vowel** says its name.

a	e	i	o	u

Say these words aloud. You'll hear that the long vowels say their names.

bike   cube   bone

train   teeth

Circle the long vowel sounds in the words. Then draw a line from the long vowel word to the matching picture.

hay

bee

pie

snow

fruit

slide

Long Vowels

A **long vowel** says its name.

a   e   i   o   u

Write the long vowel word that matches each picture.

＿ ＿ ＿ ＿

＿ C ＿ ＿ ＿

＿ ＿ ＿

＿ ＿ ＿ ＿

＿ ＿ ＿ f ＿ ＿ ＿

Long Vowels

a   e   i   o   u

Write the long vowel word that matches each picture above.
Then write another word that has the same long vowel sound.

u _ _ c _ _ _   _____

_ _ _   _____

_ _ n e   _____

_ l _ n _   _____

_ i _ n   _____

Long Vowels

A **long vowel** says its name.

| a | e | i | o | u |

Circle the word in each sentence that has a long vowel sound and then write the vowel sound.

1. Larry put his (coat) in the closet.   <u>long o</u>

2. The ducks were swimming in the lake.   _____

3. Three children went to the school party.   _____

4. Mary closed her book and left the room.   _____

5. That puppy is awfully cute.   _____

6. Mark painted the walls in his room red.   _____

7. Mike finished his lunch quickly.   _____

8. An elephant led the circus parade.   _____

9. The farmer will grow apples and carrots.   _____

Long Vowels

Using the words in the choice box, write the words that make the same long vowel sound.

cute	snow	time	may	make
grow	trip	see	boat	way
tube	free	mine	check	music
wide	we	bean	log	bug
~~name~~	drag	use	hive	load

Long a

name _____ _____ _____

Long e

_____ _____ _____ _____

Long i

_____ _____ _____ _____

Long o

_____ _____ _____ _____

Long u

_____ _____ _____ _____

Short Vowels

A **short vowel** does not say its name.

a   e   i   o   u

Say these words aloud. You'll hear that the short vowels don't say their names.

bug   hat   clock

bell   lips

Circle the short vowel sounds in the words. Then draw a line from the short vowel word to the matching picture.

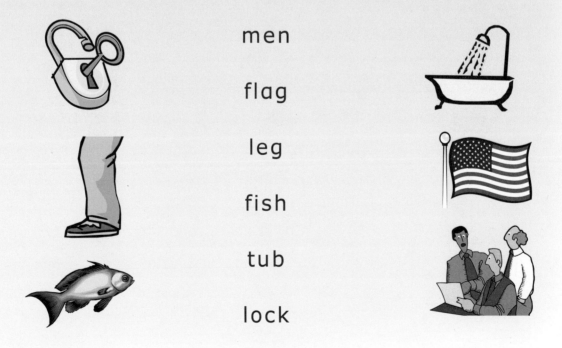

men

flag

leg

fish

tub

lock

Short Vowels

a   e   i   o   u

Write the short vowel word that matches each picture.

_ _ _

_ _ _ _

_ _ _ _

_ _ _

_ _ _

Short Vowels

A **short vowel** does not say its name.

| a | e | i | o | u |

Write the short vowel word that matches each picture above.
Then write another word that has the same short vowel sound.

__ __ x   _____

d __ __ __   _____

c __ __   _____

__ __ d   _____

__ c h __ c k __ __   _____

Short Vowels

a   e   i   o   u

Circle the word in each sentence that has a short vowel sound and then write the vowel sound.

1. Lee likes limes, grapes, (and) rice.   _short a_

2. I see a big gray whale, Kate!   _____

3. I may race, not skate.   _____

4. Jane baked a nice apple pie.   _____

5. I see a snake on a crate.   _____

6. May I name a crane Bob?   _____

7. I hiked like Mike, but I became lame.   _____

8. I spied nine vines winding down a pine.   _____

9. Fred waves while he shaves.   _____

Short Vowels

A **short vowel** does not say its name.

| a | e | i | o | u |

Using the words in the choice box, write the words that make the same short vowel sound.

glad	wheel	shut	shed	mock	flip
twig	melt	that	nice	trot	mutt
fin	bag	jet	block	frame	mud
pack	will	bone	mug	pots	send

Short a

glad _____ _____ _____

Short e

_____ _____ _____ _____

Short i

_____ _____ _____ _____

Short o

_____ _____ _____ _____

Short u

_____ _____ _____ _____

Silent e

When a vowel and a consonant together are followed by an **e**, the **e** is silent.

at - ate

Write the word that describes each picture. Then draw a line matching the words that have changed.

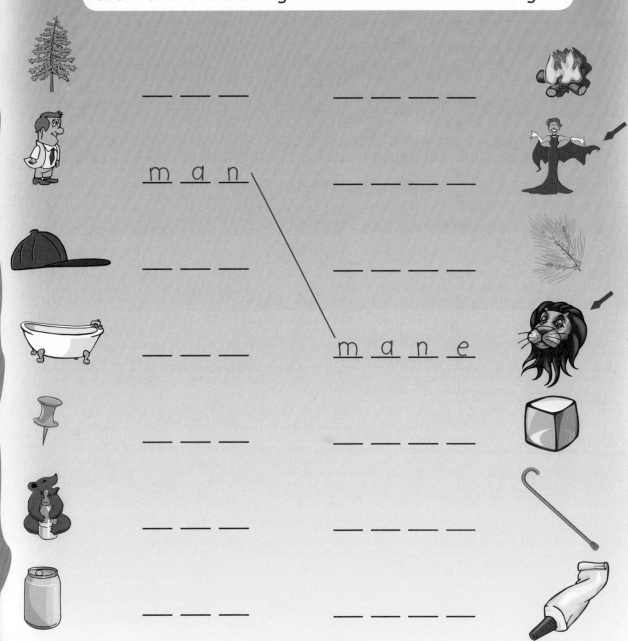

_ _ _   _ _ _ _

m a n   _ _ _ _

_ _ _   _ _ _ _

_ _ _ _   m a n e

_ _ _   _ _ _ _

_ _ _   _ _ _ _

_ _ _   _ _ _ _

Silent e

When a vowel and a consonant together are followed by an **e**, the **e** is silent.

at - ate

From the choice box, write the silent e word to finish each sentence.

phone	tire	grape	gave
tune	~~ate~~	globe	nine

1. Jim a t e dinner with his parents.

2. The car has a flat ___ ___ ___ ___.

3. Sara is eight and her friend, Tim, is ___ ___ ___ ___.

4. I located North America on the ___ ___ ___ ___ ___.

5. She handed me a ___ ___ ___ ___ ___ popsicle.

6. He played a ___ ___ ___ ___ on the piano.

7. I talked to my brother on the ___ ___ ___ ___ ___.

8. My dad ___ ___ ___ ___ me a puppy on my birthday.

Silent e

Add an 'e' to each word in the choice box to complete the sentences below.

bit   us   rob   not   mad

hug   slid   cut   ~~twin~~

1. Jerry gave his twin brother a ball of t w i n e.

2. I got mad when my mom ___ ___ ___ ___ me do my homework.

3. I bit the candy bar and then gave my brother a ___ ___ ___ ___.

4. Jane and Emily slid down the ___ ___ ___ ___ ___.

5. My mother sent a ___ ___ ___ ___ saying I was not to go outside.

6. The guy who tried to rob the bank was wearing a ___ ___ ___ ___.

7. Jason cut in line to stand next to the ___ ___ ___ ___ girl.

8. The teacher told us to ___ ___ ___ pens and not pencils on the test.

9. Ben's grandmother gave him a ___ ___ ___ ___ hug!

Silent e

When a vowel and a consonant together are followed by an **e**, the **e** is silent.

Read each sentence and circle the silent e words in each sentence.

2   1.   I saw an (ape) in a (cage) at the zoo.

3   2.   I will race you to the gate at the lake!

4   3.   Take your bike and ride to the cave.

2   4.   I hope he brings a rope.

2   5.   I ate cake for lunch.

2   6.   My kite got stuck in the tall pine.

2   7.   Two mice were in the bag of rice.

3   8.   The nose on his face was huge and red.

2   9.   I will use my cape to put out this fire!

3   10.   It was nice to skate on the ice.

R-Controlled Vowels

R-controlled vowels are vowels that change their sounds when they are followed by an **r**.

ar   er   ir   or   ur

Write the r-controlled word that matches each picture.

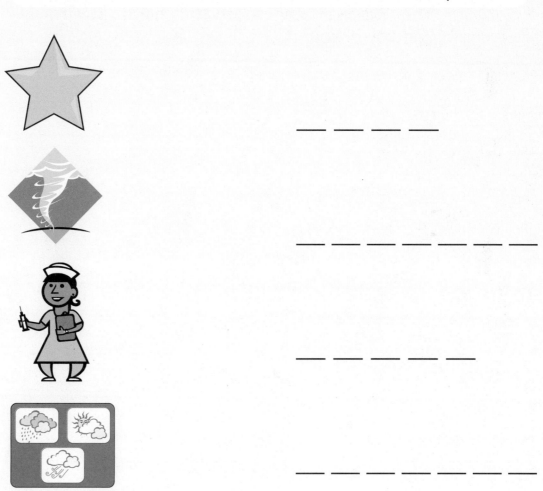

__ __ __ __

__ __ __ __ __ __

__ __ __ __ __

__ __ __ __ __ __

__ __ __ __

R-Controlled Vowels

R-controlled vowels are vowels that change their sounds when they are followed by an **r**.

| ar | er | ir | or | ur |

Write the r-controlled word that describes each picture above. Then write another word that has the same r-controlled vowel sound.

f __ __ m   _____

__ __ __ t h __ __   _____

__ __ __ d   _____

__ __ __ r   _____

__ __ r __ __ y   _____

R-Controlled Vowels

Write the word that describes the picture.
Then circle the r-controlled vowels.

   s u r f
 _ _ _ _ _ _

   _ _ _   _ _ _

   _ _ _ _   _ _ _ _ _

   _ _ _ _ _   _ k _ _ _

   _ _ _ _ _ _

 _ _ m b _ _ g _ _

R-Controlled Vowels

R-controlled vowels are vowels that change their sounds when they are followed by an **r**.

| ar | er | ir | or | ur |

Read each sentence. Then circle the words with r-controlled vowels.

3   1. The (farmer) put his (horses) in the (barn).

2   2. When it got dark, he turned on the lights.

3   3. My brother is the best soccer player on the team.

2   4. The dog had a thorn in its foot and it hurt.

3   5. John put the paper in the third drawer.

2   6. My sister plays the harp.

2   7. I like lots of butter on my corn.

3   8. He drove the large cart through the dirt.

3   9. I took a jar of water with me to the park.

R-Controlled Vowels

Write the r-controlled vowel used in two of the words. Then cross out the word that does not have the r-controlled vowel and write a new word that does.

u r	urn	~~truck~~	fur	curl
__ __	arm	card	pie	_____
__ __	claw	acorn	horn	_____
__ __	fern	flower	dime	_____
__ __	toys	bird	fir	_____
__ __	nurse	purse	pillow	_____
__ __	barn	star	grape	_____
__ __	shoulder	soccer	tape	_____
__ __	boy	fork	corn	_____
__ __	skirt	blouse	shirt	_____

Vowel Digraphs

Vowel digraphs are two vowels next to each other in which the first vowel makes the long vowel sound, and the second vowel is silent.

| ai | ay | ea | ee | ie | oa |

Write the vowel digraph word that matches each picture.

_ _ _ _

_ _ _ c h

_ _ _

_ _ _ _

_ _ _ l

_ _ _

Vowel Digraphs

ai   ay   ea   ee   ie   oa

Write the vowel digraph word that describes each picture above. Then write another word that has the same vowel digraph sound.

s _ _ _ p   _____

_ _ _ v e _   _____

_ _ _ p   _____

p l _ _ _   _____

_ n _ _ l   _____

f _ _ _ _   _____

Vowel Digraphs

Vowel digraphs are two vowels next to each other in which the first vowel makes the long vowel sound, and the second vowel is silent.

ai   **ay**   **ea**   **ee**   **ie**   **oa**

Circle the vowel digraph in each word below. Then write the long vowel sound you hear when you say the word. Then write a new word that uses the same vowel digraph.

1. br(ai)n   _____a_____   _____train_____

2. tries   _____   _____

3. boat   _____   _____

4. green   _____   _____

5. grain   _____   _____

6. boast   _____   _____

7. beach   _____   _____

8. fail   _____   _____

Vowel Digraphs

ai **ay** **ea** **ee** **ie** **oa**

Circle the vowel digraph words in each sentence.

2 1. Kenneth wanted to (stay) longer but he had to (leave.)

2 2. May wore ribbons on her braids.

2 3. His knee hurt and walking was painful.

2 4. Jeff grabbed the soap and tried to wash the dog.

3 5. I am taking a trip to the East Coast today.

3 6. The old dog always stayed by the little goat.

4 7. I need to lie on the beach and soak up some sun.

3 8. The seal swam up to the boat the next day.

3 9. I used my green crayon and red paint.

Vowel Digraphs

Vowel digraphs are two vowels next to each other in which the first vowel makes the long vowel sound, and the second vowel is silent.

| ai | ay | ea | ee | ie | oa |

Write the vowel digraph word that describes each picture. Then circle the vowel digraph.

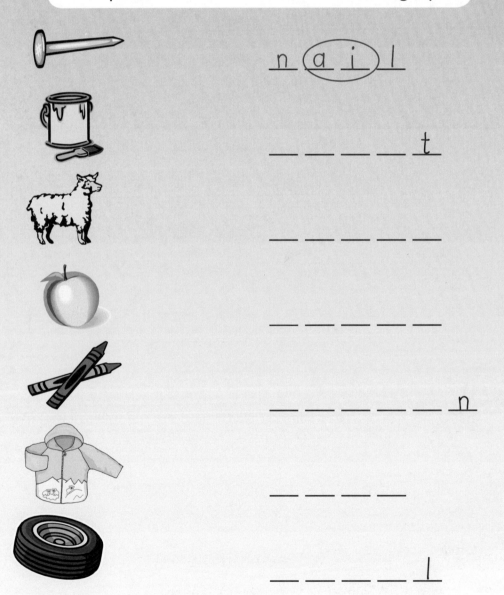

n (a i) l

_ _ _ _ t

_ _ _ _ _

_ _ _ _ _

_ _ _ _ _ n

_ _ _ _

_ _ _ _ l

Vowel Diphthongs

Vowel diphthongs are two vowels next to each other that blend together to make a sound.

au	aw	ew	oi	oo	oo	ou	ow	oy

Write the vowel diphthong word that describes each picture.

— — — — p — p — —

— — —

— — —

— r — n

— — — — d

s o i l

— — — — —

— — — —

Teaching Note: The "w" in the diphthongs ow and aw is used as a vowel.

Vowel Diphthongs

Vowel diphthongs are two vowels next to each other that blend together to make a sound.

au	aw	ew	oi	oo	oo	ou	ow	oy

Write the vowel diphthong word that describes each picture above. Then write another word that has the same diphthong sound.

s c r e w   blew

c ___ ___ ___ n   _____

___ o ___ ___   _____

___ ___ ___ s ___   _____

g ___ ___ ___ ___   _____

___ ___ l   _____

___ a ___   _____

___ ___ t ___   _____

___ ___ t   _____

Vowel Diphthongs

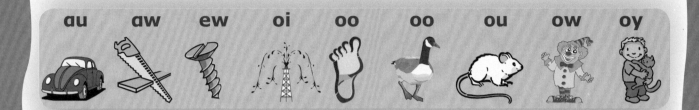

| au | aw | ew | oi | oo | oo | ou | ow | oy |

Complete the sentence with a vowel diphthong word from the choice box and circle the vowel diphthong.

book   soil   screw   ~~caught~~   broom

toys   house   frown   claws

1. Billy tossed me the ball and I c (a u) g h t it.

2. This ___ ___ ___ ___ is good for growing roses.

3. Grab a ___ ___ ___ ___ m and help me.

4. Sarah had a ___ ___ ___ ___ ___ on her face.

5. The lamp will work after I ___ c ___ ___ ___ in this lightbulb.

6. I checked a ___ ___ ___ ___ out of the library.

7. That cat has sharp ___ ___ ___ ___ ___!

8. Sadie sat down to play with her ___ ___ ___ ___.

9. It got cold, so Julie went into the ___ ___ ___ ___ ___.

Vowel Diphthongs

Vowel diphthongs are two vowels next to each other that blend together to make a sound.

| au | aw | ew | oi | oo | oo | ou | ow | oy |

Write the vowel diphthong word for each picture. Then circle the vowel diphthong.

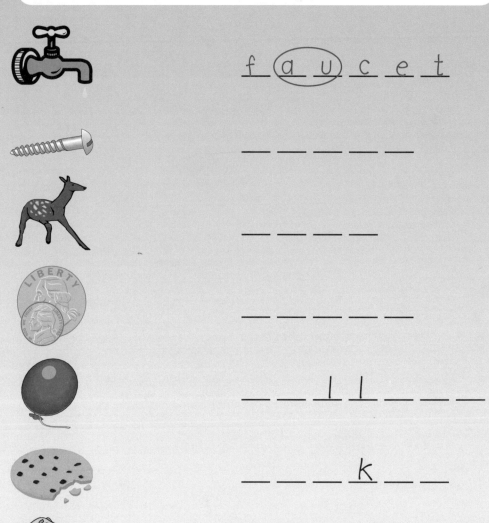

f (a u) c e t

_ _ _ _ _ _

_ _ _ _

_ _ _ _ _

_ _ _ l l _ _ _

_ _ _ k _ _

_ _ _ _

Vowel Diphthongs

au	aw	ew	oi	oo	oo	ou	ow	oy

Write the vowel diphthong word for each picture. Then circle the vowel diphthong.

p o i s o n

_ _ _ _ _

_ _ _

_ _ _ _ _

_ _ _ _ _

_ _ _ _ _

_ _ _ _ _

Single Sound Consonants

Single letter consonants make a single sound.

Write the word for each picture and then write three words that have the same beginning sound.

__ __ _s_ __

1._____

2._____

3._____

__ _a_ __ __

1._____

2._____

3._____

__ __ __ _p_ _h_ __ __

1._____

2._____

3._____

_ _ a _ m _ _ _

1._____

2._____

3._____

_ _ _ m

1._____

2._____

3._____

_ i _ _

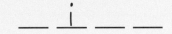

1._____

2._____

3._____

_ i _ h _

1._____

2._____

3._____

Single Sound Consonants

Single letter consonants make a single sound.

> Write the word for each picture and then write three words that have the same beginning sound.

_ _ _ n

1._____

2._____

3._____

_ _ p _

1._____

2._____

3._____

_ _ g

1._____

2._____

3._____

Consonant Blends

Consonant blends are consonants next to each other. Each consonant makes a sound.

> l **blends:** bl, cl, fl, gl, pl
> r **blends:** br, cr, dr, fr, gr, pr, tr
> s **blends:** sc, sk, sl, sm, sn, sp, sq, st, sw

> Write a consonant blend word for each picture.
> Then circle the consonant blend.

ⓢ ⓒ h o o l

_ _ _ _ _ _ _

_ _ _ _ _

_ _ _ _ _

_ _ _ _ _ _

_ _ _ _ _

_ _ _ _ _

Consonant Blends

Consonant blends are consonants next to each other. Each consonant makes a sound.

l blends: bl, cl, fl, gl, pl
r blends: br, cr, dr, fr, gr, pr, tr
s blends: sc, sk, sl, sm, sn, sp, sq, st, sw

Write the consonant blend word for each picture. Then circle the consonant blend.

c l o w n

___ ___ ___ ___ ___

___ ___ ___ ___ ___ ___

___ ___ ___ ___

___ ___ ___ ___

___ ___ ___ ___ ___

___ ___ ___ ___ ___

Consonant Blends

Write the consonant blend word for each picture.
Then circle the consonant blend.

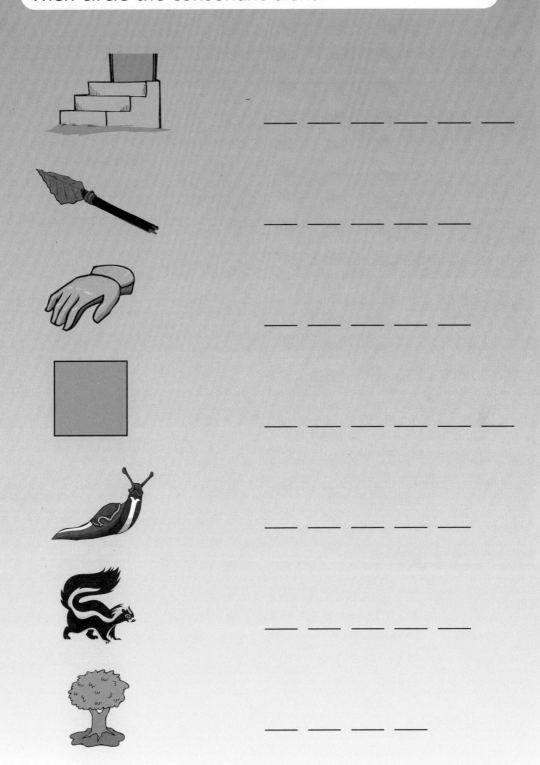

_ _ _ _ _ _ _

_ _ _ _ _

_ _ _ _ _

_ _ _ _ _ _

_ _ _ _ _

_ _ _ _ _

_ _ _ _

Consonant Blends

Consonant blends are consonants next to each other. Each consonant makes a sound.

l blends: bl, cl, fl, gl, pl
r blends: br, cr, dr, fr, gr, pr, tr
s blends: sc, sk, sl, sm, sn, sp, sq, st, sw

Complete the Word Bender™ using seven consonant blends. Change or add only the letters that go in the circles. The rest of the letters stay the same.

p r i n c e

_ ○ ○ _ ○

○ _ ○ ○ _

_ ○ ○ ○ _ ○

○ ○ ○ ○ _

_ ○ ○ ○ ○

t r e e

◯ _ ◯ ◯ STOP

_ ◯ ◯ ◯ ◯

_ ◯ ◯ ◯ ◯

_ ◯ ◯ ◯ ◯

_ ◯ ◯ ◯ ◯

_ ◯ ◯ ◯

_ ◯ ◯ ◯

Consonant Digraphs

Consonant digraphs are two consonants that are put together to form a new sound.

| ch | ck | ph | sh | th | wh |

Complete the chart by writing each consonant digraph and a _new_ word for each digraph.

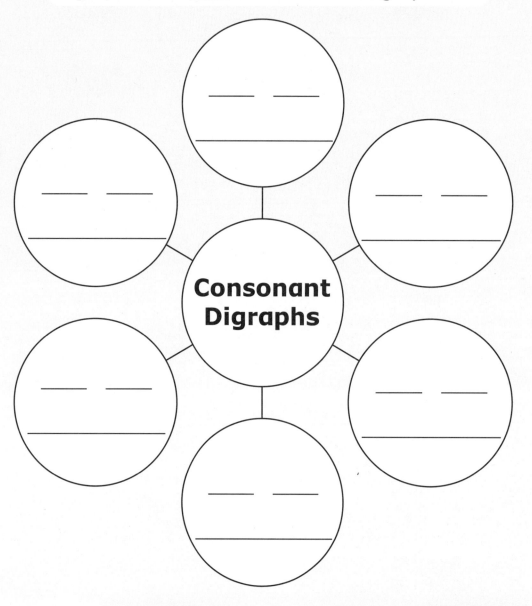

Consonant Digraphs

Consonant Digraphs

| ch | ck | ph | sh | th | wh |

Write the consonant digraph word that matches each picture.

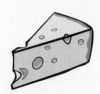

__ __ __ __ _s_ __

__ _n_ __ __

__ __ __ _p_ __ __

__ __ __ __ __ _w_

__ __ __ __

__ __ __ _s_ __ _l_ __

Consonant Digraphs

Consonant digraphs are two consonants that are put together to form a new sound.

| ch | ck | ph | sh | th | wh |

Write the word that matches each picture. Then write another word that has the same consonant digraph sound.

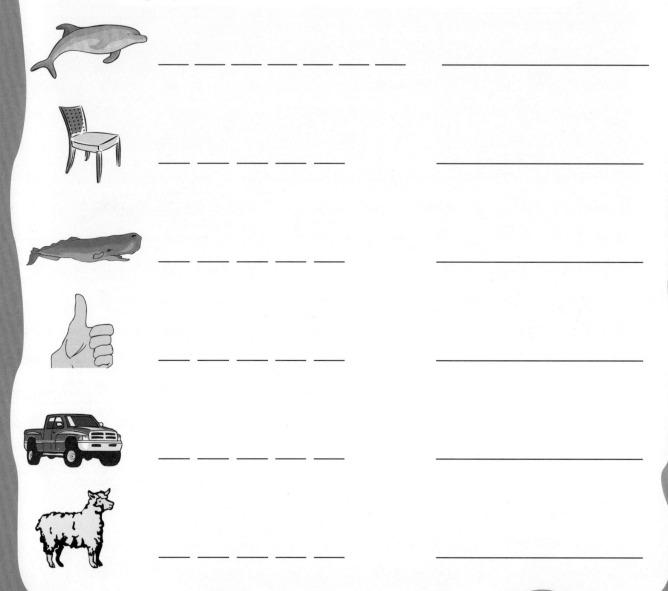

_ _ _ _ _ _ _ _   _____

_ _ _ _ _ _   _____

_ _ _ _ _   _____

_ _ _ _ _   _____

_ _ _ _ _   _____

_ _ _ _ _   _____

Consonant Digraphs

ch	ck	ph	sh	th	wh

Make "silly soup" by writing a consonant digraph word in each blank.

Find a **big**

+

One __ _l_ _e_ __ __ _a_ __ _t_

One __ __ __ __ _e_ _p_

One __ __ _i_ __ __ _e_ _n_

One __ __ __ _a_ __ _e_

One _s_ __ __ _o_ __ __

Cover with water.

Cook for __ __ __ __ _e_ _e_ days.

_Q_ _u_ _i_ __ __ _l_ _y_   add   __ __ __ __ _e_ _e_

_b_ _l_ __ __ __ _s_   of   __ __ __ __ _s_ _e_.

Consonant Digraphs

Consonant digraphs are two consonants that are put together to form a new sound.

ch	ck	ph	sh	th	wh

Have a "silly soup" party. Add a consonant digraph word in each blank.

1. __ __ __ __ _e_ your friends.

2. Ask them to join you at __ __ __ _e_ _e_

   _ó_ _c_ __ _o_ __ __ after the quiz.

3. __ __ __ _n_ your friends arrive, give them a big

   topped with __ __ _e_ _e_ __ _e_.

4. __ __ _e_ _n_ you are _f_ _i_ _n_ __ __ _e_ _d_,

   put the leftover soup in a big   .

Y as a Vowel and a Consonant

Y is used as a long vowel in some words.

fry   fly

Circle the words that use y as a long vowel.

by   gym

dry   myth

fly   spy

hymn   sty

July   fry

crypt   cyst

Y as a Vowel and a Consonant

Y is used as a short vowel in some words.

myth   hymn

Circle the words that use y as a short vowel.

(gym)   sky

shy   myth

pry   syllable

sly   Egypt

physical   pry

cry   rhythm

Y as a Vowel and a Consonant

Y is used as a consonant in some words.

yes   yellow

> Circle the words that use y as a consonant.

rhythm   (you)

fry   gym

yahoo   yolk

yummy   crypt

spy   yarn

yawn   young

Y

Syllables

Syllables are chunks of sound. All words have at least one syllable. Syllables can be just one letter or a group of letters.

> Say the word for each picture. The circles show the number of syllables in each word. Touch each circle as you say each word part slowly. Then write the word in syllables.

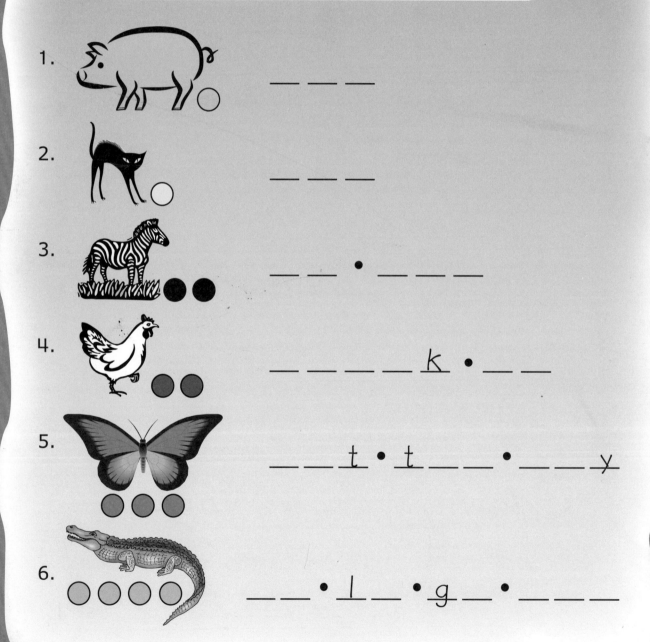

1. ___ ___ ___

2. ___ ___ ___

3. ___ ___ • ___ ___ ___

4. ___ ___ ___ ___ k • ___ ___

5. ___ ___ t • t ___ ___ • ___ ___ y

6. ___ ___ • l ___ • g ___ • ___ ___ ___

Syllables

Say the word for each instrument.
Then write the word in syllables.

1. __ __ __ __

2.  __ __ __ __

3.  __ __ __ __

4.  __ u i • __ __ __

5. __ __ • __ __ • __

6. x __ • __ • __ __ __

7. __ __ • __ __

Syllables

Syllables are chunks of sound. All words have at least one syllable. Syllables can be just one letter or a group of letters.

> Say the word to match the picture. Then write the word in syllables.

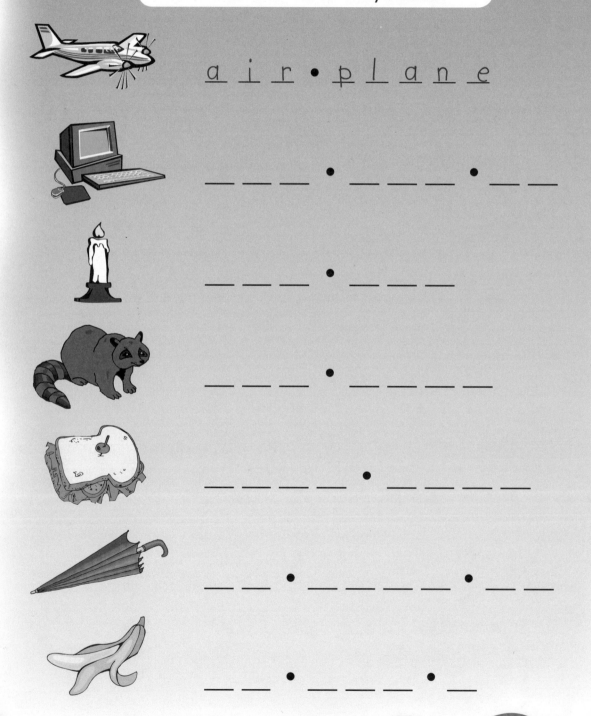

a i r • p l a n e

___ ___ ___ ___ • ___ ___ ___ • ___ ___

___ ___ ___ • ___ ___ ___

___ ___ ___ • ___ ___ ___ ___

___ ___ ___ ___ • ___ ___ ___ ___ ___

___ ___ • ___ ___ ___ ___ • ___ ___

___ ___ • ___ ___ ___ • ___

Syllables

Fill in the chart using <u>Y</u> for yes and <u>N</u> for no as you solve the puzzle.

	Mark	Debbie	Teresa	Bradley

Find each person's name.

1. The curly-haired girl has the most syllables in her

   name. _____

2. The curly-haired boy has the fewest syllables in

   his name. _____

Syllables *

Syllables are chunks of sound. All words have at least one syllable. Syllables can be just one letter or a group of letters.

Fill in the chart using <u>Y</u> for yes and <u>N</u> for no as you solve the puzzle.

Two students and two teachers have favorite fruits. Find each person's favorite fruit.

1. The name of the boy's favorite fruit has the most syllables, and Mr. Fox's fruit has the fewest syllables.

    _____   _____

2. Ms. Sharp's fruit grows larger than the girl's fruit.

    _____   _____

* For more *Mind Benders*® activities, please see our *Mind Benders*® series.

Word Families

A **word family** is a group of letters that make the same sound.

Find the word families and write the
words of each family in its box.

~~cat~~ tan mat pan rat can hat met
pet sat fan jet net ran wet

a t family

c a t

_____

_____

_____

_____

__ __ family

_____

_____

_____

_____

_____

__ __ family

_____

_____

_____

_____

_____

ten fin hip pen thin chin pin lip
den trip drip hen men slip win

__ __ family

_____

_____

_____

_____

_____

__ __ family

_____

_____

_____

_____

_____

__ __ family

_____

_____

_____

_____

_____

Word Families

A **word family** is a group of letters that make the same sound.

Find the word families and write the
words of each family in its box.

~~dog~~ cub jog mock sock hog dock
hub rock sub clock frog log rub tub

o g family

_d o g_

_____

_____

_____

_____

__ __ family

_____

_____

_____

_____

__ __ __ family

_____

_____

_____

_____

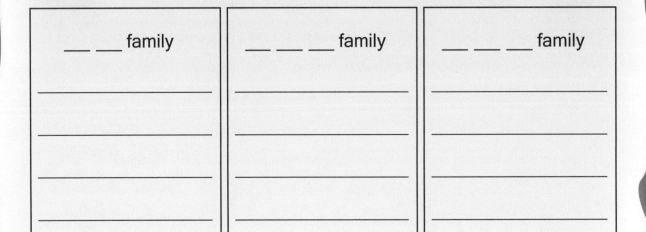

bug mug late band sand hate state
chug and mate hand lug fate rug land

__ __ family

_____

_____

_____

_____

__ __ __ family

_____

_____

_____

_____

__ __ __ family

_____

_____

_____

_____

Word Families

Write three words for each word family.

at   _f a t_   _c a t_   _b a t_

an   _____   _____   _____

et   _____   _____   _____

en   _____   _____   _____

in   _____   _____   _____

ip   _____   _____   _____

og   _____   _____   _____

ock   _____   _____   _____

ub   _____   _____   _____

ug   _____   _____   _____

Word Families

A **word family** is a group of letters that make the same sound.

Find the word families and write the words of each family in its box.

sale gate best jest pale late male nest
date whale mate pest rest gale rate

__a__ __l__ __e__ family

__sale__

____ ____ ____ family

____ ____ ____ family

bite fine ride dine bride write line white
hide side pine polite mine tide site

____ ____ ____ family

____ ____ ____ family

____ ____ ____ family

Word Families

bake thrill sleep pill sheep cake weep
will lake fill take beep wake hill deep

_a_ _k_ _e_ family

_b a k e_

___ ___ ___ family

___ ___ ___ family

---

sheet clock lump dump sweet knock block feet
plump beet mock grump bump shock fleet

___ ___ ___ family

___ ___ ___ family

___ ___ ___ family

Word Families

A **word family** is a group of letters that make the same sound.

Write three words for each word family.

ake	_bake_	_cake_	_lake_
ale	_____	_____	_____
ate	_____	_____	_____
eep	_____	_____	_____
est	_____	_____	_____
ide	_____	_____	_____
ill	_____	_____	_____
ine	_____	_____	_____
ite	_____	_____	_____
ock	_____	_____	_____

High Frequency Words

High frequency words are the words used most often.

Circle seven color words.

blue

brown   why

write   white

yellow   red

black   wish

please   your

green

Write the color words in alphabetical order from a-z.

_b_ _l_ _a_ _c_ _k_

_ _ _ _ _

_ _ _ _ _

_ _ _

_ _ _ _ _

_ _ _ _ _ _

High Frequency Words

High frequency words are the words used most often.

Circle five number words.

five   three   their

four   there

one   2   1   three

to   two

win   too

so   thank

Write the number words in order, from lowest to highest.

<u>o n e</u>

___ ___ ___

___ ___ ___ ___

___ ___ ___ ___

___ ___ ___ ___

Write the number words in order, from highest to lowest.

<u>f i v e</u>

___ ___ ___ ___

___ ___ ___ ___ ___

___ ___ ___

___ ___ ___

High Frequency Words

Two words that are totally different are opposites.

Draw a line to connect nine opposites.

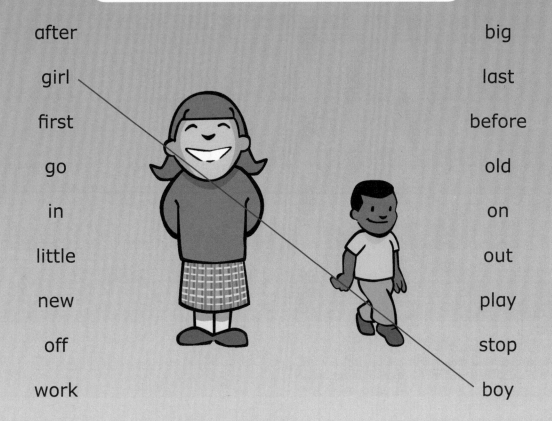

after	big
girl	last
first	before
go	old
in	on
little	out
new	play
off	stop
work	boy

Write three pairs of the opposites you identified above that could be used to describe the picture.

_____   _____

_____   _____

_____

High Frequency Words

High frequency words are the words used most often.

Alphabetize the following groups of words.

1. _____

2. _____

3. _____

4. _____

5. _____

6. _____

around	went
funny	because
sleep	don't

for	buy
look	right
always	were

1. _____

2. _____

3. _____

4. _____

5. _____

6. _____

1. _____

2. _____

3. _____

4. _____

5. _____

6. _____

soon	which
and	round
very	think

High Frequency Words

Alphabetize the following groups of words.

1. _____

2. _____

3. _____

4. _____

5. _____

6. _____

going	me
please	any
those	our

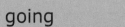

up	open
pretty	into
we	an

1. _____

2. _____

3. _____

4. _____

5. _____

6. _____

1. _____

2. _____

3. _____

4. _____

5. _____

6. _____

could	as
know	not
over	is

Contractions

Contractions are shortened words. An apostrophe (') is used in place of the missing letters.

	Contraction
I will	I'll
you will	you'll
they will	they'll
we will	we'll
she will	she'll
he will	he'll

> Use the examples above to write the two words used in each contraction.

1. I'll be there soon.   I will

2. You'll see us.   ___ ___ ___   ___ ___ ___ ___

3. She'll go with you.   ___ ___ ___   ___ ___ ___ ___

4. He'll go, too.   ___ ___   ___ ___ ___ ___

5. They'll go with us.   ___ ___ ___ ___   ___ ___ ___ ___

6. We'll go.   ___ ___   ___ ___ ___ ___

Contractions

Contraction	
would not	wouldn't
is not	isn't
are not	aren't
cannot	can't
do not	don't

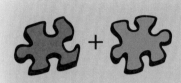 

Use the examples above to change two words in each sentence to a contraction. Then write a new sentence using the contraction.

1. He is not here. i s n ' t

   She isn't home.

2. They cannot wait. __ __ __ ‾ __

   _____

3. They do not see us. __ __ __ ‾ __

   _____

4. I would not go. __ __ __ __ __ ‾ __

   _____

5. They are not here. __ __ __ __ ‾ __ __

   _____

6. She is not here. __ __ __ ‾ __

   _____

Contractions

Contractions are shortened words. An apostrophe (') is used in place of the missing letters.

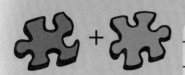

Contraction	
you have	you've
they have	they've
we have	we've

Use the examples above to change two words in each sentence to a contraction. Then write a new sentence using the contraction.

1. You have been there. __Y o u ' v e__

_____

2. They have been there. __ __ __ __ __ ‾ __ __

_____

3. We have been there. __ __ ‾ __ __

_____

4. You have done that. __ __ __ ‾ __ __

_____

5. They have done that. __ __ __ __ __ ‾ __ __

_____

6. We have done that. __ __ ‾ __ __

_____

Contractions

	Contraction			Contraction
you are	you're		she is	she's
they are	they're		he is	he's
we are	we're		it is	it's

Change two words in each sentence to a contraction. Then write a new sentence using the contraction.

1. You are correct.   __ __ __ ⁻ __ __

   _____

2. They are correct.   __ __ __ __ ⁻ __ __

   _____

3. We are all correct.   __ __ ⁻ __ __

   _____

4. He is incorrect.   __ __ ⁻ __

   _____

5. She is incorrect.   __ __ __ ⁻ __

   _____

6. It is incorrect.   __ __ ⁻ __

   _____

Contractions

Contractions are shortened words. An apostrophe (') is used in place of the missing letters.

Add the word from the choice box that forms the contraction.

am	are	have
is	not	will

are + _____ = aren't   they + _____ = they've

can + _____ = can't   they + _____ = they're

do + _____ = don't   we + _____ = we've

he + _____ = he's   we + _____ = we're

I + _____ = I'll   who + _____ = who's

I + _____ = I'm   would + _____ = wouldn't

it + _____ = it's   you + _____ = you'll

she + _____ = she's   you + _____ = you've

Contractions

Write the two words used for the contraction.

aren't = _____ + _____   they're = _____ + _____

can't = _____ + _____   they've = _____ + _____

don't = _____ + _____   we're = _____ + _____

he's = _____ + _____   we've = _____ + _____

I'll = _____ + _____   who's = _____ + _____

I'm = _____ + _____   wouldn't = _____ + _____

it's = _____ + _____   you'll = _____ + _____

she's = _____ + _____   you've = _____ + _____

   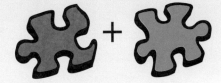

Compound Words

A **compound word** is formed when two words are joined to form a new word.

+ = bedtime

Combine two words to form a compound word.

1. _ _ _ _ _ + 🏐 = _b_ _ _ _ _b_ _ _ _l_

2. 🛏 + _ _ _ _ _ = _b_ _ _ _r_ _ _ _m_

3. 🐝 + _ _ _ _ _ = _b_ _ _h_ _ _v_ _

4. _ _ _ _ _ _ + 🐦 = _b_ _ _ _ _ _k_ _b_ _ _ _

5. 📕 + _ _ _ _ _ = _b_ _ _ _ _m_ _ _ _k_

6. 🐄 + _ _ _ _ = _c_ _ _ _ _ _ _y_

Compound Words

 = firewood

Combine two words to form a compound word.

1. + = d _ _ _ _ b _ _ l

2. + = _ _ e _ l _ _ _ s _ s

3. + = _ _ _ _ e _ _ y

4. + = _ _ o w _ _ p _ _

5. + = _ _ o _ _ a _ _

6. + = g o _ _ f _ _ h

Compound Words

A **compound word** is formed when two words are joined to form a new word.

+ = pigpen

Combine two words to make a compound word.

1. + = _n_ _ _t_ _ _b_ _ _ _ _ _

2. + = _ _ _i_ _ _ _ _ _ _w_

3. + = _ _ _g_ _ _ _i_ _

4. + = _r_ _ _ _ _c_ _ _ _ _

5. + = _ _ _ _ _ _r_

6. + = _ _o_ _ _ _u_ _ _

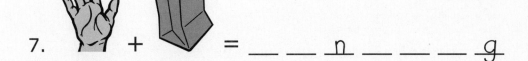

7. + = _ _ n _ _ _ g

8. + = _ _ _ _ _ b _ a _ _

9. + = p _ _ c _ _ _

10. + = _ _ n _ s h _ _ _ _

11. + = _ _ n _ b _ _ _

12. + = _ _ g _ _ h _ _ _ _

13. + = _ u _ _ l _ _ _ _ _

14. + = _ t _ _ _ _ _ s _

Compound Words

A **compound word** is formed when two words are joined to form a new word.

 = snow + flake

Write the two words that make a compound word.

1. = __ y __ + __ __ __ s __ e __

2. = b __ __ __ ' __ + __ __ e

3. = __ __ e __ __ + ⊥ __ __ __ __ __

4. = __ __ o __ + __ __ ⊥ __

5. = __ __ d __ + __ __ g

6. = __ a __ __ + __ __ x

7. = _ _ t _ _ _ r + _ l _

8. = _ _ s _ _ _ t + _ _ l _

9. = _ h _ _ _ + _ _ r _ _ _

10. = r _ _ _ + _ _ w

11. = _ _ t _ _ + _ u _

12. = _ _ _ t _ + b _ _ _ _

Synonyms

Synonyms are two words that have the <u>same</u> or almost the same meanings.

Synonyms

bug	↔	insect
pail	↔	bucket
car	↔	auto
small	↔	tiny

Fill in each blank with the best synonym from the choice box.

sad angry big ~~fall~~ gift giggle happy summer
birthday mitt nice pal raise weep small

1. autumn   _fall_ _____

2. cry   _____

3. friend   _____

4. glad   _____

5. glove   _____

6. kind   _____

7. large   _____

8. laugh   _____

9. lift   _____

10. mad   _____

11. present   _____

Synonyms

Fill in each blank with the best synonym from the choice box.

| lock bag close easy creep frighten ill |
| shout nap noise rock ~~stay~~ wealthy rest |

1. remain _____stay_____

2. rich _____

3. sack _____

4. scare _____

5. shut _____

6. sick _____

7. simple _____

8. sleep _____

9. crawl _____

10. sound _____

11. stone _____

Shades of Meaning

Some words mean about the same thing, but not exactly the same thing. The small differences in meaning are called **shades of meaning**.

That rock is big.   That rock is huge.   That rock is enormous.

Write each group of words in order, from the weakest to strongest.

1. smacked, hit, smashed

_____   _____   _____

2. grumpy, furious, mad

_____   _____   _____

3. brilliant, clever, smart

_____   _____   _____

4. tiny, small, microscopic

_____   _____   _____

5. yelled, said, roared

_____   _____   _____

6. perfect, OK, good

_____   _____   _____

Shades of Meaning

7. moist, wet, soggy

_____   _____   _____

8. messy, dirty, filthy

_____   _____   _____

9. terrible, bad, awful

_____   _____   _____

10. ask, beg, request

_____   _____   _____

11. speedy, quick, fast

_____   _____   _____

12. thin, scrawny, slim

_____   _____   _____

13. evil, mean, unkind

_____   _____   _____

Antonyms

Antonyms are two words that have opposite meanings.

Antonyms

up	↔	down
good	↔	bad
on	↔	off
yes	↔	no

Fill in each blank with the best antonym from the choice box.

teen asleep cold back full in little first
warm new night open sad soft tall top sorry

1. awake _____asleep_____

2. front _____

3. big _____

4. bottom _____

5. closed _____

6. day _____

7. empty _____

8. happy _____

9. hard _____

10. hot _____

11. old _____

Antonyms

Smile is the antonym of frown.

Fill in each blank with the best antonym from the choice box.

water day empty float ~~front~~ happy hard closed
light short out small smile stand up well wet tiny

1. back   _front_

2. down   _____

3. dry   _____

4. frown   _____

5. full   _____

6. in   _____

7. large   _____

8. night   _____

9. open   _____

10. sad   _____

11. sick   _____

12. sink   _____

Writing Detective®

Read the story, and then answer the questions based on the best evidence in the story.

How Did She Know?

[1]On Monday at school, Jaime was trying to tell her friend, Lynn, about the movie she had seen. [2]She told her it wasn't just funny. [3]She said it was really funny!

[4]The next day, Lynn saw Jaime again, and Jamie had seen another movie. [5]Lynn asked her if that movie had been funny.

[6]"No, this movie was scary. [7]I wasn't just scared, I..."

[8]Lynn stopped her. [9]"You were terrified, weren't you?"

[10]"Yes, that's right, but how did you know?"

Reading Questions

1. What sentence tells you how funny the movie was? _____

2. What sentence tells you what kind of movie the second movie was? _____

3. What three sentences tell how Jamie felt about the second movie?
_____   _____   _____

4. Number the events from 1—4 in the order they happened in the story.

   _____   Lynn said her friend was terrified.

   _____   Jaime told Lynn about a movie that made her laugh.

   _____   Lynn asked Jaime if the second movie was funny.

   _____   Jaime said the second movie frightened her.

Read the questions and write the answers in complete sentences.

1. Who is the story about? _____

_____

_____

2. What were they doing? _____

_____

_____

3. Where did this happen? _____

_____

_____

4. When did this happen? _____

_____

_____

5. How were the movies different? _____

_____

_____

Prefixes

Prefixes are a group of letters added to the beginning of words to create new words.

Prefix	Prefix Meaning	Word	New Word
dis-	not, opposite of	appear	disappear
extra-	beyond	ordinary	extraordinary
mis-	wrong	take	mistake
non-	not, no	electric	nonelectric
over-	more than needed, above	coat	overcoat

Add the correct prefix, then draw a line to match the new word with its definition.

Words

Definitions

___ ___ ___ conduct

do not agree

___ ___ ___ agree

to work too much

___ ___ ___ ___ ___ ordinary

wrong behavior

___ ___ ___ sense

fantastic or amazing

___ ___ ___ ___ work

does not make sense

Prefixes

Prefix	Meaning
dis-	not, opposite of
extra-	beyond
mis-	wrong
non-	not, no
over-	more than needed, above

Add one of the above prefixes to each word below. Then use the word in a sentence.

1. <u>e</u> <u>x</u> <u>t</u> <u>r</u> <u>a</u> terrestrial: beyond the earth

   <u>Do you believe in extraterrestrial beings?</u>

2. __ __ __ __ cook: to cook too much

   _____

3. __ __ __ trust: without trust

   _____

4. __ __ __ understand: wrong understanding

   _____

5. __ __ __ violent: not violent

   _____

Suffixes

Suffixes are a group of letters added to the end of words to create new words.

Suffix	Suffix Meaning	Word	New Word
-er	one who	farm	farmer
-ful	full of	care	careful
-less	without	hair	hairless
-able	able to	work	workable
-ment	act of	excite	excitement

Add one of the above suffixes to each word below. Then draw a line to match the new word with its definition.

Words

help __ __

wonder __ __ __

hope __ __ __ __

break __ __ __ __

enjoy __ __ __ __

Definitions

able to be broken

the act of enjoying

one who helps

full of wonder

without hope

Suffixes

Suffix	Meaning
-er	one who
-ful	full of
-less	without
-able	able to
-ment	act of

Add a suffix to each word below, and then use the word in a sentence.

1.　teach _e_ _r_ : one who teaches

   She is a good teacher.

2.　depend ___ ___ ___ ___ : able to be depended upon

   _____

3.　help ___ ___ ___ ___ : without help

   _____

4.　grate ___ ___ ___ : full of gratitude

   _____

5.　commit ___ ___ ___ ___ : act of committing

   _____

Roots

Roots are the words that prefixes and suffixes are attached to.

Root	Meaning	Suffix	Meaning
depend	to place trust	-ment	the act of
help	to give assistance	-er	one who
excite	to stir up	-ful	full of
teach	to instruct	-able	able
hope	to wish for something	-less	without

Write the missing words by combining a suffix and a root that match each meaning.

Meanings

_ _ _ _ _ _ _   one who educates

_ _ _ _ _ _ _ _ _ _   trustworthy

_ _ _ _ _ _ _ _ _ _   stirring to activity

_ _ _ _ _ _ _ _ _   dependent

_ _ _ _ _ _ _ _   full of promise

Roots

Prefix	Meaning	Root	Meaning
over-	excessive, above	agree	to grant consent
mis-	wrong	terrestrial	relating to the earth
dis-	not, opposite of, excluding	work	labor
extra-	beyond	trust	having confidence in one

Write the missing words by combining a prefix and a root that match each meaning.

Meanings

_ _ _ _ _ _ _ _   not to agree

_ _ _ _ _ _ _ _   to work too hard

_ _ _ _ _ _ _ _   to be suspicious of

_ _ _ _ _ _ _ _ _ _ _ _ _

beyond the earth

Capitalization

Capitalize holidays, months, and days of the week.

Add the beginning capital letter to each word.
Then write the word in the correct column.

___ecember
___ather's ___ay
___hristmas
___emorial ___ay
___ew ___ear's ___ay
___ndependence _ay
___olumbus ___ay
___other's ___ay
___residents' ___ay
___une

___ebruary
___ednesday
___alloween
___anuary
___arch
___unday
___aturday
___ctober
___eptember
___hanksgiving

___hursday
___onday
___ovember
___pril
___riday
___uesday
___ugust
___uly
___aster

Holidays	Months	Days of the Week

Capitalization

Circle the words that should be capitalized.
Then answer the questions.

Solomon Grundy

Solomon Grundy,
Born on (monday,)
Christened on tuesday,
Married on wednesday,
Took ill on thursday,
Worse on friday,
Died on saturday,
Buried on sunday.
This is the end
Of Solomon Grundy.

What day did Solomon Grundy get sick?

Thursday

What day was there a wedding?

— — — — — — — — —

What day was Solomon Grundy's christening?

— — — — — — — — —

What was the day of Solomon Grundy's birth?

— — — — — — —

What was the day of Solomon Grundy's death?

— — — — — — — —

What day was Solomon Grundy put in the ground?

— — — — — — —

What day did Solomon Grundy get worse?

— — — — — — —

Capitalization

Capitalize holidays, months, and days of the week.

Circle the words that should be capitalized. Then answer the questions.

Thirty Days Hath September

Thirty days hath september,
april, june, and november;
february has twenty-eight alone,
All the rest have thirty-one,
Excepting leap year, that's the time
When february's days are twenty-nine.

How many months are in a year? _____

Which months have 31 days?

_____ _____ _____ _____

_____ _____ _____

Which months have 30 days?

_____ _____ _____

Which month has 28 or 29 days?

_____

Capitalization

Capitalize the first word of a sentence.

My name is Rob.

Capitalize the pronoun I.

Jan and I went to a movie.

Capitalize proper names - person's name, nickname, initials, and titles and their abbreviations.

Rob, Robby, R., Doctor, Dr.

Capitalize proper nouns and their abbreviations, groups, titles of books, and names of places.

Boy Scouts, *Stuart Little*, New York, N.Y.

Circle the words that should be capitalized.

2 1. tuesday is my birthday and i am excited.

2 2. My name is robert and my nickname is bob.

3 3. My dad's name is sam g. brown.

3 4. I go to dr. larry smith.

2 5. I am a boy scout.

3 6. "Little red riding hood" is my favorite tale.

2 7. The united states is my home.

Capitalization

Capitalize the first word of a sentence.

My name is Rob.

Capitalize the pronoun I.

Jan and I went to a movie.

Capitalize proper names - person's name, nickname, initials, and titles and their abbreviations.

Rob, Robby, R., Doctor, Dr.

Capitalize proper nouns and their abbreviations, groups, titles of books, and names of places.

Boy Scouts, *Stuart Little*, New York, N.Y.

Capitalize days of the week, months and holidays.

| Monday, Tuesday, Wednesday | January, February, March, April, May, June, July | New Year's Day, Thanksgiving |

Circle 23 letters that should be capitalized.

my name is thomas and my nickname is buddy. my next birthday will be on christmas day, tuesday, december 25. i live in the united states. my dad is sam g. smith. he works with the boy scouts. my mother is dr. janet smith. she works at the hospital.

Capitalization

Write a story that tells about you. Include examples of all the rules on page 92.

_____

_____

_____

_____

_____

_____

_____

_____

_____

_____

Editor in Chief®

Circle 17 letters that should be capitalized.

mary is my sister. she goes to kennedy elementary school and her teacher's name is susan a. jones. tomorrow is memorial day and mary and i are going on a picnic with my friend, rocky. on tuesday, we will read "cinderella."

Circle 16 letters that should be capitalized.

new year's day is january 1. my family always goes skiing on mount baler. my ski instructor's name is tony s. brown. i like him. he brings his dog, fido, with him. he and i play in the snow.

Sentences

A **sentence** is a group of words that form a complete thought.

Write a sentence about each picture.

1. <u>The boy threw the football.</u>

2. _____

3. _____

4. _____

5. _____

Sentences

A **sentence** is a group of words that form a complete thought. A sentence fragment is only part of a sentence. It is not a complete thought.

The shark.   Swims in the ocean.

The shark swims in the ocean.

Use each fragment to create a complete sentence.

1. Sharks are good. Swimmers in the ocean.

_____

_____

2. I like to. Go to the ocean to swim.

_____

_____

3. I like to. Play in the ocean.

_____

_____

Sentences

A run-on sentence is two or more complete sentences that should be separate sentences.

Grant is a good student he got all A's.

To correct this type of run-on sentence, follow two steps:
1. Place a period after the first complete sentence.
2. Capitalize the first word of the new sentence.

Grant is a good student. He got all A's.

Correct each run-on sentences by creating two sentences.

1. Jim is a good student he got all B's.

_____

_____

2. Tom is an average runner Tom is faster than Lee.

_____

_____

3. Pam is taller than Maria Pam is shorter than Nel.

_____

_____

Sentences

A sentence fragment is only part of a sentence. It is not a complete sentence. Complete sentences must have a noun (subject) and a verb (predicate).

Write a sentence fragment about each picture.

_____

_____

Use each of your fragments to create a complete sentence.

_____

_____

Sentences

A run-on sentence is two or more complete sentences that should be separate sentences.

Grant is a picky eater he does not like vegetables.

To correct this type of run-on sentence, follow two steps:
1. Place a period after the first complete sentence.
2. Capitalize the first word of the new sentence.

Grant is a picky eater. He does not like vegetables.

Correct each run-on sentence by creating two sentences.

1. Grant is a picky eater he does not like carrots.

_____

_____

2. Grant is a picky eater he does not like peas.

_____

_____

3. Grant is a good reader he likes stories about sports.

_____

_____

Sentences

A run-on sentence is two or more complete sentences that should be separate sentences.

Correct each run-on sentence by creating two sentences.

1. I like to go to the park we play ball.

_____

_____

2. I like to go to the pool we swim all day.

_____

_____

3. I like to go to the store we always buy gum.

_____

_____

Sentences

A run-on sentence can also be a sentence using the word "and" to join more than one idea that should be separate sentences.

Grant is a good eater and he likes vegetables.

Think about where one idea ends and another begins. To correct this type of run-on sentence, make two separate sentences.

1. Cross out the "and" you don't need.
2. Put a period in place of the "and."
3. Capitalize the first word in the new sentence.

Grant is a good eater. He likes vegetables.

Correct each run-on sentence by creating two sentences.

1. Grant is a good eater and he likes corn.

_____

_____

2. Grant is a good swimmer and he likes racing.

_____

_____

3. Grant is good at math and he likes to subtract.

_____

_____

Sentences

1. A sentence fragment is an incomplete sentence. Complete sentences must have a noun (subject) and a verb (predicate).
2. A run-on sentence is two or more complete sentences that should be separate sentences.
3. A run-on sentence can also use the word "and" to join more than one idea that should be separate sentences.

Identify which sentences below are run-ons and which are fragments. Then rewrite each sentence correctly.

1. Grant is a good eater he like carrots. _____run-on_____

 _____Grant is a good eater._____

 _____He likes carrots._____

2. Grant is a good hiker he likes to hike. _____

 _____

 _____

3. I like to go to the park and we play ball. _____

 _____

 _____

4. I like to play. In the park. _____

 _____

 _____

5. I like to swim. In the ocean. _____

 _____

 _____

Subject and Predicate

A sentence has two main parts:
The **subject** tells who or what the sentence is about.
The **predicate** tells what is happening.

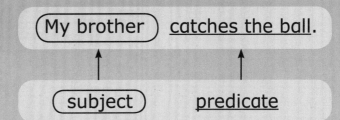

My brother catches the ball.

subject   predicate

Write a sentence for each picture. Circle the (subject) and underline the predicate.

_____

_____

_____

_____

_____

_____

_____

_____

_____

Subject and Predicate

A sentence has two main parts:
   The **subject** tells who or what the sentence is about.
   The **predicate** tells what is happening.

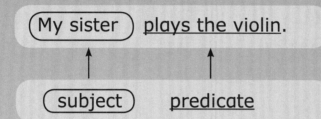

Write a sentence for each picture. Circle the (subject) and underline the predicate.

_____

_____

_____

_____

_____

_____

_____

_____

_____

Subject and Predicate

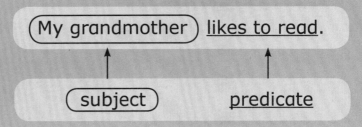

Circle the (subject) and underline the predicate in each sentence.

1. A funny person made us laugh.

2. Jim and I like to play.

3. A mean dog tried to bite me.

4. Jim and I like to climb trees.

5. Jim tells lots of jokes.

6. My brother and I have two little puppies.

Paragraphs

A **paragraph** is a group of sentences dealing with one subject. The first sentence of a paragraph is always indented.

My favorite pet is a cat. They have cute faces and soft fur. I love the way they purr when I pet them. If I had a cat of my own, I'd be very happy.

1. A paragraph has a topic sentence, which gives the main idea.

My favorite pet is a cat.

2. A paragraph has supporting details.

They have cute faces and soft fur.

I love the way they purr when I pet them.

3. A paragraph has a closing sentence.

If I had a cat of my own, I'd be very happy.

Write a paragraph about your favorite holiday.

Topic sentence: _____

_____

Supporting detail: _____

_____

Supporting detail: _____

_____

Closing sentence: _____

_____

Paragraphs

Write a paragraph about your favorite food.
Then draw a picture of your favorite food.

My Favorite Food Is _____

Topic sentence: _____

_____

Supporting detail: _____

_____

Supporting detail: _____

_____

Closing sentence: _____

_____

Paragraphs

A **paragraph** is a group of sentences dealing with one subject. The first sentence of a paragraph is always indented.

> Write a paragraph about your favorite animal.
> Then draw a picture of your favorite animal.

_____

_____

_____

_____

_____

_____

Paragraphs

Write a paragraph about the picture. Be sure to indent the first sentence of the paragraph. Write a topic sentence, supporting details, and a closing sentence.

_____

_____

_____

_____

_____

_____

_____

_____

Paragraphs

A **paragraph** is a group of sentences dealing with one subject. The first sentence of a paragraph is always indented.

Write a paragraph about the picture. Be sure to indent the first sentence of the paragraph.
Write a topic sentence, supporting details, and a closing sentence.

_____

_____

_____

_____

_____

_____

_____

Paragraphs

This paragraph is scrambled! Write the numbers of the topic sentence, supporting detail sentences, and the closing sentence. Then write the paragraph correctly.

My Best Birthday Party

¹We swam and took turns jumping in and splashing! ²The best birthday party I ever had was when I turned six. ³Then we had cake and I got some great presents. ⁴It was the best party ever! ⁵My mom and dad took my friends and me to the swimming pool.

_____ Topic sentence

_____ Supporting sentence

_____ Supporting sentence

_____ Supporting sentence

_____ Closing sentence

My Best Birthday Party

_____

_____

_____

_____

_____

_____

_____

Nouns

A **common noun** is a person, place, or thing.

The boy is a noun.

Find another noun in the picture.

_____

The box is a noun.

Find another noun in the picture.

_____

The astronaut is a noun.

Find 2 more nouns in the picture.

_____

_____

The book is a noun.

Find 3 more nouns in the picture.

_____

_____

_____

Nouns

Write a sentence for the picture using at least one common noun. Then circle the common noun(s) in your sentence.

1.  The (boy) rode on his (skateboard.)

2.

3.

4.

5.

Nouns

A **proper noun** is a particular or special person, place, or thing. It is always capitalized.

Lilly Baker (Person)

California (Place)

Hillcrest School (Thing)

Read the sentences and circle the proper nouns.

1   1. (Adam) is holding a cat.

2   2. Maryanne kicked the ball to Lynn.

3   3. Jeremy went to see Dr. Scott.

1   4. Tina loves to feed the birds.

2   5. Bobby ate all of Fred's dessert.

1   6. The band played at Mary's party.

Nouns

Circle the common nouns and underline the proper nouns in the sentences.

2 1. <u>James</u> likes to paint (pictures.)

2 2. Susan has three dogs.

2 3. Kendell lives in that house.

2 4. My cat caught a mouse.

2 5. The chicken crossed the road.

3 6. Larry ate a peach and a pear.

2 7. Monica went to the Jackson Park.

2 8. Two men got off the bus.

Nouns

A **common noun** is a person, place, or thing.
A **proper noun** is a particular or special person, place, or thing. It is always capitalized.

Put the common nouns and proper nouns from the choice box in the correct list.

monkey   Peterson School   skateboard   Billy
spoon   baby   balloon   library   Jon   store
rock   tree   teacher   outside   California
kitchen   brother   doctor   park   Zoe
book   apple   mother   office

Person	Place	Thing
mother	store	monkey

Nouns

Write a sentence for each picture using a common noun or a proper noun. Then circle the noun.

1. **Proper Noun**

(Evan) likes to go swimming.

_____

_____

2. **Common Noun**

_____

_____

_____

3. **Common Noun**

_____

_____

_____

4. **Common Noun**

_____

_____

5. **Proper Noun**

_____

_____

Pronouns

A **pronoun** is a word that can take the place of a noun.

Bill has a dog.   He has a dog.

Read the sentence and circle the noun. Then write a new sentence, replacing the noun with a pronoun from the choice box. You may use a pronoun more than once.

they   she   he   it

1. (Pam) fixed lunch today. _She fixed lunch today._

   _____

2. Bob, Bill, and Ted went to the park. _____

   _____

3. The pillow is soft. _____

   _____

4. Jason went fishing. _____

   _____

5. Molly loves chocolate. _____

   _____

6. Anna and Grace play soccer. _____

   _____

Pronouns

Circle the pronoun in each sentence.

1. (He) drinks hot cocoa.

2. It is a cute puppy.

3. She ate an apple.

4. They like to skate.

5. He will go to school tomorrow.

6. I can't wait for vacation.

7. We want to see that movie.

8. It is small and yellow.

9. Did they catch the bus?

Pronouns

A **pronoun** is a word that can take the place of a noun.

A noun is a person, place, or thing.

Bill has a dog.
Sue has a dog.
Bill and Sue have a dog.
I love Oregon!

A pronoun is a word that can take the place of a noun.

He has a dog.
She has a dog.
They have a dog.
I love it!

Circle the pronoun in each sentence.

1. (He) ate a peanut butter and jelly sandwich.

2. They like peanut butter and jelly sandwiches.

3. He is hungry.

4. She likes to eat peanut butter and jelly sandwiches.

5. He has a peanut butter and jelly sandwich every day.

6. Toby thinks making them is easy.

7. We all like to eat peanut butter and jelly sandwiches.

Verbs

A **verb** is a word that shows action.

The boy holds the cat.

Holds shows action, so holding is a verb.

The box walked.

Walked shows action, so walked is a verb.

The teacher read the book.

Write another verb from the picture.

The students $\underline{l}$ $\underline{}$ $\underline{}$ $\underline{t}$ $\underline{}$ $\underline{n}$.

Write a verb for the sentence below.

The dog $\underline{}$ $\underline{u}$ $\underline{}$ $\underline{s}$.

Verbs

A **verb** is a word that shows action.

Write a sentence using a verb for each picture and then circle the verb.

1. The boy (rode) on his skateboard.

2.

3.

4.

5.

Verbs

Write a sentence using a verb for each picture and then circle the verb.

1. 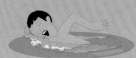 He (swam) in the lake. _____

2.  _____

3.  _____

4.  _____

5.  _____

Verbs

A **verb** is a word that shows action.

> Circle the verb in the sentence. Then write another sentence using the same verb.

1. Mark (walks) to school every morning.

   Mary walks her dog every day.

2. The runners raced to the finish line.

   _____

3. The old dog snoozes in the sun.

   _____

4. The teacher read the book to the class.

   _____

5. The children laughed at the clowns.

   _____

6. Jennifer slipped on the icy sidewalk.

   _____

7. Jacob threw the ball to Sam.

   _____

Verbs

Use a verb from the choice box to fill
in the blank in each sentence.

ran   climbed   ~~yelled~~   swam
flew   dreamed   listened

1. Jeremy ___yelled___ to his friends to wait up.

2. At the picnic, most of the children _____ in
   the lake.

3. Last night, I _____ I was a race car driver.

4. The two girls _____ the tree and ate
   apples.

5. The students _____ carefully to the
   teacher.

6. Lucy _____ to her bedroom to get a sweater.

7. The swallows _____ through the air.

Verbs

A **verb** is a word that shows action.

Write a sentence about the picture using the verb.

1.

ran

All the children ran to the park.

2.

laughed

3.

yell

4.

eats

5.

scrubbed

6.

flew

Verb Tenses

Verb tenses tell when the action takes place.

> Present tense is what is happening.
> I eat bananas.
>
> Past tense is what happened.
> I ate a banana yesterday.

Underline the verb in each sentence and circle whether it is present tense or past tense.

1. I <u>ride</u> my bike on the sidewalk.   (Present)   Past

2. The boys rode their bikes to school.   Present   Past

3. My mother baked cookies for us.   Present   Past

4. I walk to my grandmother's house.   Present   Past

5. Morgan laughed at the clowns.   Present   Past

6. The puppy drinks the milk.   Present   Past

7. I buy lots of books.   Present   Past

8. The cat climbed the tree.   Present   Past

Verb Tenses

Verb tenses tell when the action takes place.

Present tense is what is happening.
I eat bananas.

Past tense is what happened.
I ate a banana yesterday.

Complete each sentence with a verb from the choice box and circle whether it is present tense or past tense.

sings   munch   broke   watched   chews   wash
walk   blew   roared   plays   climbed

1. I ___ ___ ___ ___ ___ on potato chips.   Present   Past

2. Tim ___ ___ ___ ___ ___ ___ ___ a movie.   Present   Past

3. I ___ ___ ___ ___ my face every morning.   Present   Past

4. The coach ___ ___ ___ ___ his whistle.   Present   Past

5. Sam ___ ___ ___ ___ ___ ___ ___ the tree.   Present   Past

6. Jason ___ ___ ___ ___ ___ soccer.   Present   Past

7. The lion ___ ___ ___ ___ ___ ___ ___.   Present   Past

8. I ___ ___ ___ ___ to school.   Present   Past

9. The dog ___ ___ ___ ___ ___ the bone.   Present   Past

10. Jim ___ ___ ___ ___ ___ the window.   Present   Past

11. Leah ___ ___ ___ ___ ___ very well.   Present   Past

Verb Tenses

Present tense is what is happening.
I eat bananas.

Past tense is what happened.
I ate a banana yesterday.

Future tense is what will happen.
I will eat a banana tomorrow.

Using the words in the choice box, write the correct verb tense for each sentence. Each word can be used only once.

jump   jumped   jumps

1. My cat _____ at the toy mouse I bought.

2. She will _____ at it tomorrow, too.

3. She has _____ every time I have shown it to her.

smiles   smile   smiled

1. My grandmother _____ whenever she sees me.

2. She _____ when I stopped by last week.

3. I know she will _____ when she sees me tomorrow.

scream   screams   screamed

1. My cousin _____ every time she sees a spider.

2. She _____ the last time she saw one.

3. I'm sure she will _____ when she sees another one.

Verb Tenses

Complete each clue by changing the red present tense verb to a past tense verb. Then complete the crossword puzzle.

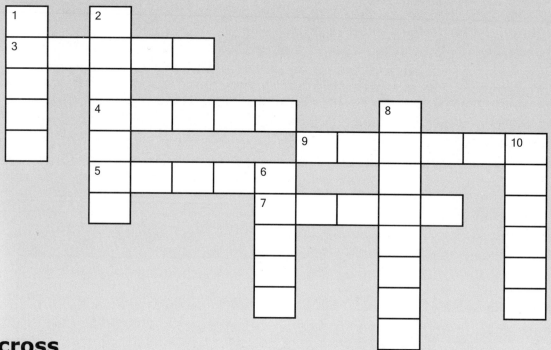

Across

3. I dare _____ my brother to climb the tree.

4. I gaze _____ up at the stars in the sky.

5. The teacher end _____ the lesson and left the room.

7. The girl race _____ to school because she was late.

9. James pet _____ the little puppy.

Down

1. On the test, I add _____ the rows of numbers.

2. Cody drag _____ the sled up the hill.

6. Nathan dry _____ the dishes.

8. Emily attend _____ the concert last night.

10. I dust _____ the books on my shelf.

Subject-Verb Agreement

Subject-verb agreement is using a singular verb with a singular subject and using a plural verb with a plural subject.

The lady sings.

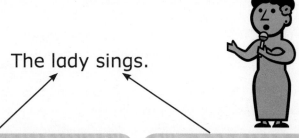

Lady is a singular subject.   Sings is a singular verb.

The children sing.

Children is a plural subject.   Sing is a plural verb.

Read each sentence and circle the correct subject and verb to match the picture.

The bird - birds   fly - flies .

The bird - birds   eats - eat .

Subject-Verb Agreement

Subject-verb agreement is using a singular verb with a singular subject and using a plural verb with a plural subject.

Read each sentence and circle the correct verb.

1. The boy play - (plays) with a truck.

2. He play - plays with trucks.

3. They play - plays with trucks.

4. The girl play - plays with trucks.

5. She play - plays with a truck.

6. They play - plays with trucks.

7. The girl and the boy play - plays with trucks.

Subject-Verb Agreement

Read each sentence and circle the correct verb.

1. The zebra is - are over there.

2. The pigs is - are over there.

3. The snake is - are over there.

4. The zebras is - are over there.

5. The pig is - are over there.

6. The snakes is - are over there.

7. The snake and the pig is - are over there.

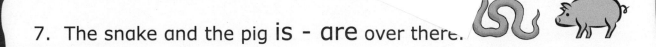

8. The zebras and the pigs is - are over there.

Writing Detective®

Read the story and then answer the questions based on the best evidence in the story.

Recipe For Disaster

[1]It was a rainy Sunday afternoon, and Allison decided to bake some cookies. [2]Her brother, Mike, came in to the kitchen.

[3]"I'm making peanut butter cookies," Allison replied. [4]"Want to help?"
[5]"Sure," he said. [6]"I'll read the directions to you while you mix stuff up."

[7]Mike was watching a baseball game so he turned on the TV on the counter and grabbed the cookbook. [8]"Three cups of flour," he read. [9]"Two cups of sugar. [10]One teaspoon of baking soda."

[11]Just then, there was a roar from the crowd at the game. [12]"Now add one teaspoon of homerun," Mike told Allison, as he watched the TV.

[13]"Mike, give me the cookbook," Allison said. [14]"I'll read it myself."

[15]Looking puzzled, Mike gave her the cookbook. [16]"What did I do?" he wondered to himself.

Reading Questions

1. What sentence tells you the kind of cookies Allison is going to make? _____

2. What sentence tells you what happened when the crowd roared? _____

3. Why do you think Allison took the cookbook from Mike?

_____

   What sentence is the best evidence for your answer? _____

4. Number the events from 1 – 5 in the order they happened in the story.

   ____ There is a roar from the crowd at the baseball game.

   ____ Allison decides to make some cookies.

   ____ Mike tells Allison to add a teaspoon of homerun.

   ____ Mike comes into the kitchen.

   ____ Allison asks Mike for the cookbook.

Writing Detective®

Now that you've read the story and answered the questions, write a paragraph about what the story was about. Before you write your paragraph, look at the questions and make some notes about the story to guide you when you write.

1. Who is the story about? _____

2. What were they doing? _____

3. Where did this happen? _____

4. When did this happen? _____

5. How did the baseball game affect Mike's reading? _____

_____

_____

_____

_____

_____

_____

_____

_____

_____

Adjectives

An **adjective** is a word that describes a noun (person, place, or thing) or a pronoun. It gives more information about the noun or pronoun.

I ate the big apple.

Circle the adjectives in each sentence.

2 1. My bike is (blue) and Jake has a (green) bike.

2 2. The little bear ate the juicy berries.

3 3. The old man smiled at the cute little baby.

2 4. The two deer munched on the tender leaves.

2 5. I bought one ticket to the scary movie.

2 6. Nathan grabbed the big shovel, but I wanted one that was small.

2 7. The two girls watched as the three kittens played with the string.

3 8. He ate two sandwiches and a big red tomato.

2 9. Five cows munched on the green grass.

Adjectives

Circle the adjective in the sentence. Then write another sentence using the same adjective.

1. The (little) turtle ate some lettuce.

She sat on the little stool.

_____

2. My big toe hurts.

_____

_____

3. I ate the purple plum.

_____

_____

4. My mother made some chocolate pudding.

_____

_____

5. Janell has three sisters.

_____

_____

6. The graceful swan glided across the lake.

_____

_____

Adjectives

When comparing two things, add er to most words.

> Bill is taller than Amy.

Sometimes the word more is added in front of words with three or more syllables.

> Amy has more difficult chores than Bill.

When comparing three or more things, add est to most words.

> Bill is the tallest.

Sometimes the word most is added in front of words with three or more syllables.

> Amy has the most difficult chores.

Use special words to compare things that are good or bad.

> good - better - best   or   bad - worse - worst

Fill in the blanks for each sample sentence.

1. His hair is _s_ _h_ _o_ __ _t_ __ __ than mine is.

2. This race is __ __ __ __ important.

3. Carl has the _s_ __ _o_ _r_ _t_ __ __ __ hair.

4. Amy has the __ __ __ __ beautiful hair.

5. I am a __ _o_ _o_ _d_ reader, but Pat reads

   __ _e_ _t_ _t_ _e_ _r_. Carl is the __ _e_ _s_ _t_ reader.

   Janet is a __ _a_ _d_ reader. Sam is __ _o_ _r_ _s_ _e_ than

   Janet. Tom is the __ _o_ _r_ _s_ _t_ reader.

Adjectives

Read each sentence and circle the correct word.

1. Today's test is **more - most** important than yesterday's.

2. Her pencil is **shorter - shortest** than mine.

3. Carl has the **shorter - shortest** pencil.

4. Amy has the **more - most** beautiful handwriting.

5. I am the **good - best** speller.

6. Of the three sisters, Penny is the **older - oldest**.

7. Jeremy is **taller - tallest** than I am.

8. I'm wearing the **warmer - warmest** coat I have.

9. This is the **more - most** delicious pizza I've ever eaten.

10. Today's game was **more - most** exciting than last week's game.

Adjectives

When comparing two things, add er to most words.

> Bill is taller than Amy.

Sometimes the word more is added in front of words with three or more syllables.

> Amy has more difficult chores than Bill.

When comparing three or more things, add est to most words.

> Bill is the tallest.

Sometimes the word most is added in front of words with three or more syllables.

> Amy has the most difficult chores.

Use special words to compare things that are good or bad.

> good - better - best   or   bad - worse - worst

Read each sentence and circle the correct word.

1. Pat spells best - better than I.

2. Yesterday's test was more - most important than today's.

3. Yesterday's test was the more - most important test of the year.

4. Sam spelled more - most words correctly than Tom.

5. Sam is the good - best speller in my class.

Adjectives

Use the chart to complete the story.

	Brad	Mike	Beth	Kate
Tennis	bad	best	good	worst
Height	tallest	short	shortest	tall

__ __ __ __ is the __ e __ __ tennis player, but

__ __ __ __ is also __ __ o __.

__ __ __ __ __ is the __ __ r __ __ tennis player

because she is the only player __ __ __ __ can beat.

M __ __ __ is __ __ l l __ __ than

__ e __ __, but both of them are __ __ __ __ __ e __

than B __ __ __ and __ __ __ __. __ __ t __ is

the __ __ __ __ __ __ __ __.

Editor in Chief®

In the story, write the correct adjectives in the spaces. Circle the spelling error and write the correction above the error.

The **Big** Game

2 best, 1 most, 1 worst, 1 shorter, 1 spelling

Today's game was _____ than yesterday's

game. Sam hit a grand slam! He is the _____

player. We were not surprised that Tom did not even hit

the ball. He is the _____ baseball player,

but he's really good at playing soccer. The _____

important game of the hole season is tomorrow. I will be the

_____ player in that game!

Adverbs

An **adverb** describes a verb. Most adverbs end with –ly.
An adverb answers questions:

When?	Molly ran yesterday.
How?	Molly ran quickly.

Underline the verb and circle the adverb in each sentence.

1. Lucas (quietly) <u>opened</u> the front door.

2. Patty happily hugged her grandfather.

3. The crowd cheered loudly.

4. The cows must be milked daily.

5. The fish swam slowly around the pool.

6. Nick pays his bills monthly.

7. The man yelled angrily at the boys.

8. Sarah will call tomorrow.

9. Jamie slurped his soda loudly.

10. The baby slept peacefully in his crib.

Adverbs

An **adverb** describes a verb. Most adverbs end with –ly.
An adverb answers questions:

| When? | Molly ran yesterday. |
| How? | Molly ran quickly. |

> Circle the adverb in the sentence. Then write another sentence using the same adverb.

1. The cows moved (slowly) toward the barn.

   My grandmother walked slowly down the stairs.

2. We went to the park yesterday.

   _____

   _____

3. The woman yelled loudly at her children.

   _____

   _____

4. The cat ran quickly up the tree.

   _____

   _____

5. Alex does his homework nightly.

   _____

   _____

Adverbs

6. Sara walked carefully on the icy sidewalk.

_____

_____

7. The swan glided gracefully across the pond.

_____

_____

8. The three boys spoke quietly to each other.

_____

_____

9. My uncle visited us recently.

_____

_____

_____

10. Suddenly, the car veered off the road.

_____

_____

11. The phone rang twice before I could answer it.

_____

_____

Singular and Plural

To change a noun from **singular** (one) to **plural** (more than one), add an "s" to the end of most words.

boat → boats

For words ending in y, change the y to i and add es.

berry → berries

For words ending in s, ss, sh, ch, x, and sometimes o, add es.

dish → dishes

A few words do not follow these rules.

fish → fish

Write the plural of each word.

1.  horse

___ ___ ___ ___ ___ ___

2. bunny

___ ___ ___ ___ ___ ___ ___

3. dish

___ ___ ___ ___ ___ ___

4. deer

___ ___ ___ ___

Singular and Plural

Write the plural word for each picture.

m o n k e y s

_ i r _ _

_ u _ _

_ o _ _

_ _ i _ _

_ a _ _

Singular and Plural

To change a noun from **singular** (one) to **plural** (more than one), add an "s" to the end of most words.

boat → boats

For words ending in y, change the y to i and add es.

berry → berries

For words ending in s, ss, sh, ch, x, and sometimes o, add es.

dish → dishes

A few words do not follow these rules.

fish → fish

Change each word from singular to plural.

cake ___ ___ ___ ___ ___

door ___ ___ ___ ___ ___

dress ___ ___ ___ ___ ___ ___ ___

family ___ ___ ___ ___ ___ ___ ___ ___

cow ___ ___ ___ ___

wife ___ ___ ___ ___ ___

lady ___ ___ ___ ___ ___

ox ___ ___ ___ ___

mess ___ ___ ___ ___ ___ ___

mouse ___ ___ ___ ___ ___

school ___ ___ ___ ___ ___ ___ ___

apple   __ __ __ __ __ __

baby   __ __ __ __ __ __

box   __ __ __ __ __

book   __ __ __ __ __

bunny   __ __ __ __ __ __ __

city   __ __ __ __ __ __

kiss   __ __ __ __ __ __

lock   __ __ __ __ __

lunch   __ __ __ __ __ __

shelf   __ __ __ __ __ __ __

party   __ __ __ __ __ __

picnic   __ __ __ __ __ __

tomato   __ __ __ __ __ __ __

sky   __ __ __ __

story   __ __ __ __ __ __ __

Singular and Plural

To change a noun from **singular** (one) to **plural** (more than one), add an "s" to the end of most words.

boat → boats

For words ending in y, change the y to i and add es.

berry → berries

For words ending in s, ss, sh, ch, x, and sometimes o, add es.

dish → dishes

A few words do not follow these rules.

fish → fish

Change each word from plural to singular.

ponies   __ __ __ __

children   __ __ __ __ __

girls   __ __ __ __

sheep   __ __ __ __ __

geese   __ __ __ __ __

potatoes   __ __ __ __ __ __

deer   __ __ __ __

leaves   __ __ __ __

teeth   __ __ __ __ __

women   __ __ __ __

buses   __ __ __

chips   __ __ __ __

zebras   __ __ __ __ __

foxes   __ __ __

dreams   __ __ __ __ __

families   __ __ __ __ __ __

fish   __ __ __ __

kisses   __ __ __ __

ladies   __ __ __ __

lakes   __ __ __ __

classes   __ __ __ __ __

boxes   __ __ __

bushes   __ __ __ __

banjos   __ __ __ __

Singular and Plural

To change a noun from **singular** (one) to **plural** (more than one), add an "s" to the end of most words.

boat → boats

For words ending in y, change the y to i and add es.

berry → berries

For words ending in s, ss, sh, ch, x, and sometimes o, add es.

dish → dishes

A few words do not follow these rules.

fish → fish

Change each word from singular to plural.

boy   __ __ __ __

foot   __ __ __ __

bus   __ __ __ __ __

peach   __ __ __ __ __ __ __

car   __ __ __ __

child   __ __ __ __ __ __ __

dream   __ __ __ __ __ __

flag   __ __ __ __ __

mix   __ __ __ __ __

book   __ __ __ __ __

dish   __ __ __ __ __

hero   __ __ __ __ __

tooth   __ __ __ __ __

life   __ __ __ __ __

kiss   __ __ __ __ __ __

man   __ __ __

boss   __ __ __ __ __ __

wish   __ __ __ __ __

dog   __ __ __ __

ball   __ __ __ __ __

tuna   __ __ __ __

beach   __ __ __ __ __ __

puzzle   __ __ __ __ __ __ __

cake   __ __ __ __ __

circus   __ __ __ __ __ __ __ __

cat   __ __ __ __

Singular and Plural

To change a noun from **singular** (one) to **plural** (more than one), add an "s" to the end of most words.

boat ➞ boats

For words ending in y, change the y to i and add es.

berry ➞ berries

For words ending in s, ss, sh, ch, x, and sometimes o, add es.

dish ➞ dishes

A few words do not follow these rules.

fish ➞ fish

Change each word from plural to singular.

girls   — — — —

prefixes   — — — — — —

lunches   — — — — —

men   — — —

wishes   — — — —

echoes   — — — —

cakes   — — — —

balls   — — — —

mice   — — — — —

Editor in Chief ®

Circle the errors in each story and write the corrections above the errors.

A Weary Wait

6 verb tense, 2 subject-verb agreement, 2 spelling

Carol slowly walks to the corner after soccer practice yesterday and waits for the bus. There were three other girls waiting and they was sitting on a bench. Carol were tired and asked if she could sit down, too. One of the girls stands up to give Carol her spot on the bench. Just then, the bus arrives, so Carol had to weight until she was on the bus before she finally sits down. She was so tried that she puts her head back on the seat and fell fast asleep.

A Trip to the Farm

3 singular/plural, 3 verb tense, 1 subject-verb agreement, 3 spelling

The second-graders was visiting a farm. The students saw horses and chikens. There were six cows and seven sheeps. The students walked down the hill to a creek, where they see frogs and fishes. They went to the orchard, wear they picked apples that were plump and juicy. The farmer showed them a pen where several calfs were sleeping in the hey. The students get to pet some lambs, too. Then they climb back on the bus for the long ride back to school.

Periods

Use a **period** after an abbreviation. An abbreviation is a shorter way of writing a word or group of words.

January	Monday	Street	Mister
Jan.	Mon.	St.	Mr.

Write a period at the end of the abbreviation.

I saw a rabbit at Sixteen Apple Ave
A cat lives at Fourteen Red Rd
Someone's aunt lives at Fifteen Pot Ct
Twelve Bay Dr is the home of a coyote.
Nineteen Stinky Ln is a skunk's happy home.

Use the picture clues and choice box to complete the addresses. Do not use abbreviations.

Avenue	Lane	Court
Drive	Road	

 1 9 _ t _ _ _ y _ _ _ _

 _ _ _ _ _ _ _ _ _ _

 _ _ _ _ _ _ _ _ _ _

 _ _ _ _ _ _ _ _ _ _

 _ _ _ _ _ _ _ _ _ _

Periods

Write a period at the end of each abbreviation.

On Mon my sister had a bowl of applesauce.
On Tues my brother had a whole pie.
On Wed my dad had an apple.
On Thurs my mom had a hamburger.
On Fri my grandmother had a popsicle.
On Sat my grandfather had a carrot.
On Sun my dog had a bone.

Use the picture clues to complete the chart. Do not abbreviate.

Monday   Tuesday   Wednesday
Thursday   Friday   Saturday   Sunday

Family Member	Day	Food
	_ _ _ _ _ _	
	_ _ _ _ _ _	
	_ _ _ _ _ _	
	_ _ _ _ _	
	_ _ _ _ _ _ _	
	_ _ _ _ _ _ _	
	_ _ _ _ _ _	

Periods

Months can be abbreviated.

Fill in the blanks to show the abbreviated or spelled way of writing dates.

January 1, 2012

__ __ __. 1, 2012

March 1, 2013

__ __ __ . 1 , 2 __ __ __

__ __ __ __ __ __ 1, __ __ __ __

Aug. 1, 2011

September 1, 2012

__ __ __ __ . 1 , __ __ __ 2

__ __ __ __ __ ber __, 2 __ __ __

Dec. 1, 2013

Periods

When using abbreviations, remember that three months are not abbreviated because they are too short (May, June, and July).

Complete the Word Bender™, using abbreviations or complete words for the months. Change or add only the letters that go in the circles. The rest of the word stays the same. The number of the month is listed beside each clue.

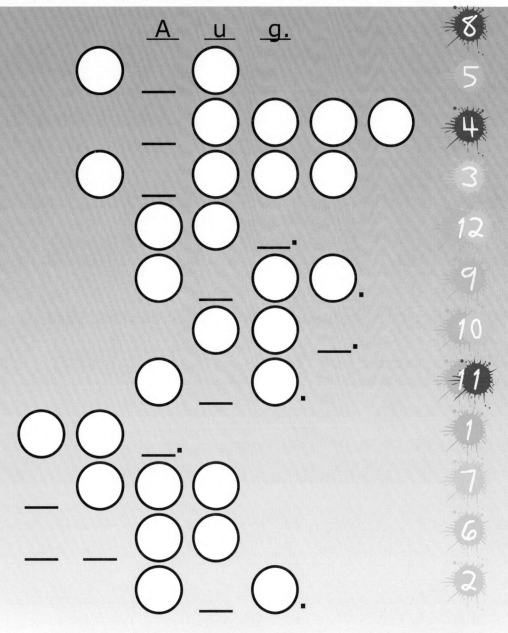

A   u   g.

8
5
4
3
12
9
10
11
1
7
6
2

Periods

Use a **period** to end a telling (declarative) sentence.
My name is Sam Adam White.

Use a **period** after initials.
My initials are S.A.W.

Use 4 periods, and 12 initials to fill in the blanks.

My name is Susan Anne White___   My initials are ___. ___. ___.

His name is Tom Ulysses Black__   His initials are ___. ___. ___.

William David White is his name___   His initials are ___. ___. ___.

I am John Adam Smith___   My initials are ___. ___. ___.

Create names for these initials.

S. A. D. _____

D. O. G. _____

B. A. D. _____

initial   abbreviation   name

Use the words from the choice box to complete the sentence.

An __ __ __ __ __ __ __ is an

__ __ __ __ __ __ __ __ __ __ __ __

of a ___ ___ ___ ___.

Question Marks

Use a **question mark** (?) after a direct question.

Is the puppy lost?

Put a question mark at the end of each direct question.
Put a period at the end of each telling sentence.

1. When will lunch be ready _?_

2. Will you meet me at the library____

3. The library is closed today ____

4. We should open the door ____

5. Should we open the door ____

6. The puppy barked at me ____

7. Are you sure this is the right book ____

8. Who spilled the milk ____

9. Where do you live ____

Question Marks

Use a **question mark** (**?**) after a direct question.

Write a question about each picture.

1. *Do you like to play soccer?*

2.

3.

4.

5.

6.

Commas

Use a **comma** to separate the street address, city, and state.

I live at 111 Shaw Street, Ames, Iowa.

Use a **comma** between the day of the month and the year.

My dad was born Aug. 19, 1980.

Use a **comma** to separate items in a series.

Bring a coat, scarf, and mittens.

Add commas to the sentences.

2 1. He lives at 123 Happy Place Atlanta Georgia.

3 2. Put the plates bowls cups and napkins on the table.

1 3. Today is January 10 2007.

2 4. I live at 456 Win Avenue Weed California.

1 5. Yesterday was January 9 2011.

2 6. I went on vacation on Monday July 9 2008.

2 7. I'll get the hammer saw and nails.

2 8. I have a red ball a blue ball and a white ball.

2 9. The party was at 1010 Oak Street Dallas Texas.

Commas

Use a **comma** before a conjunction (and, but, or, so) to join two simple sentences.

Using a comma and a conjunction from the choice box, combine the two simple sentences and write a new sentence. You may use a conjunction more than once.

and   but   or   so

1. I need to study. I'll go to my room.

   _____

   _____

2. Freddy likes spaghetti. He doesn't like spinach.

   _____

   _____

3. Will you go to the party? Will you stay home?

   _____

   _____

4. I got really sleepy. I went to bed.

   _____

   _____

5. I like to play the piano. I don't play very well.

   _____

   _____

6. You can have pizza. You can have a hamburger.

   _____

   _____

Quotation Marks

Use **quotation marks** at the beginning and end of a direct quote. The first word of a quotation is capitalized.

"This is my cat."

Use a comma to separate the speaker from the quotation.

Jax said, "This is my cat."

Punctuation marks go inside the quotation marks.

Jax asked, "Is this your cat?"

Add capital letters, quotation marks, and commas to the sentences.

1. He said, "Let's go into the kitchen."

2. He yelled, get out of here! The boat is sinking!

3. I said she knows that we are late.

4. James asked is it time to go to the dentist?

5. Jacob said go away. I am trying to sleep.

6. She said there are seven dogs in my yard.

7. Mary said stop playing and come in for lunch.

8. we're having hot dogs she said.

9. the red rose is the prettiest Ellen said.

Quotation Marks

Use **quotation marks** at the beginning and end of a direct quote.

> Add capital letters, quotation marks, and commas to the sentences.

1. Dad said go to bed.

2. I have a cold and feel rotten mike said.

3. I want to eat my lunch early she said.

4. I won the game she said.

5. wow! I made the honor roll Bill said.

6. I live at 6 green St. Nel said.

7. Kim said, my favorite colors are red, green, and blue.

8. Janet said i am a good student at school.

9. My name is jim, and I am visiting he said.

10. Ian asked Is today Jan. 1, 2011?

11. Ann said, our flag is red white and blue.

12. He shouted throw me the ball!

13. Wow! James won the race Emily yelled.

14. Mike lives in atlanta Bob said.

15. J. T. said math is my best subject.

16. the test was hard Jennifer said.

17. I said mr. jones is my teacher.

18. Megan asked who was first?

19. Tim said the game is cancelled.

20. let's go to the park Gary said.

21. I was born on may 1, 1997 Sue said.

Quotation Marks

Use **quotation marks** at the beginning and end of a direct quote.

> Rewrite each sentence correctly using quotation marks, capital letters, and commas.

1. Bobby asked is it time yet?

   <u>Bobby asked, "Is it time to go yet?"</u>

2. Brett said we won't leave for an hour.

3. that kitten is cute said Devon.

4. he also has a dog Jenny said.

5. go lie down and rest said his mother.

6. this fudge is good said Mike.

7. Sam asked did you eat it all.

8. Jenna said i was born on may 13 2000.

Editor in Chief®

Add punctuation, commas, and capital letters to the story. Then circle the errors and write the corrections above the errors.

Dog Gone

6 sets of quotation marks, 6 commas,
8 capital letters, 2 verb tense

rover ran away James said.

His sister asked are you sure?

yes. I look in the backyard and he isn't there. he isn't in the garage and he isn't in his doghouse james said.

His sister asked did you look in our house?

no James said.

He went to the house and climb the steps. He opened the front door. Then he turned to his sister and he had a big smile on his face.

rover is in the house said James.

Exclamation Marks

Use an **exclamation mark** (!) after a word that shows excitement.

Hooray!   Yippee!

Add a period and/or an exclamation mark to each sentence.

1. "Wow____" yells Bobby____   5. "Help____" she cried____

2. Billy yelled, "Stop____"   6. Jim shouted, "Wait____"

3. "Yikes____" she shouted____   7. "Wait____" she shouted.

4. "Yes____" he exclaimed____   8. "No____" he exclaimed____

Write three sentences with a word that shows excitement.

1._____

_____

_____

2._____

_____

_____

3._____

_____

_____

Exclamation Marks

Add a period and/or an exclamation mark to each sentence.

1. "Oh, wow____" he said____

2. He exclaimed, "There's an alligator in here____"

3. He cried, "Get me some bandages____"

4. "I'm scared____" she cried____

5. "I love it____" he exclaimed____

6. He exclaimed, "Get out of the way ____"

7. He yelled, "We just won the lottery ____"

8. "Stop____" she cried____

Write three sentences. Each sentence should include a word that shows excitement.

1._____

_____

2._____

_____

3._____

_____

Writing Detective®

Read the story and then answer the questions based on the best evidence in the story.

A Special Visitor

[1]Amber Babcock and her elephant, who was wearing a pink dress, walked down the hall and into Mrs. Cole's classroom.

[2]"Good morning, Amber," the teacher said. [3]"How are you today? [4]Is this your friend? [5]Is she a new student?" [6]Mrs. Cole wore big, thick glasses, and she peered over them as she talked to Amber.

[7]"Oh, she's just visiting," Amber replied. [8]And with that, she and the elephant took their seats.

[9]Soon, the bell rang and Mrs. Cole asked Amber to introduce her visitor. [10]"This is my friend, Ella," Amber said.

[11]The students were quiet and they watched Ella and Amber all day. [12]"I don't think I've ever had such quiet students," Mrs. Cole marveled to herself. [13]"We should have visitors every day!"

Reading Questions

What sentence tells you what the elephant was wearing? _____

What sentence tells you the elephant's name ? _____

Why do you think Mrs. Cole thought the elephant was a student?

_____

What sentence is the best evidence for your answer? _____

Number the events from 1 – 5 in the order they happened in the story.

____ Amber and the elephant take their seats.

____ Amber and her elephant walked down the hall.

____ The students were quiet and watched Amber and the elephant.

____ Mrs. Cole asked Amber if the elephant was a new student.

____ Amber said the elephant's name was Ella.

Writing Detective®

Now that you've read the story and answered the questions, write a paragraph about what the story was about. Before you write your paragraph, look at the questions and make some notes about the story to guide you when you write.

1. Who is the story about? _____

2. What were they doing? _____

3. Where did this happen? _____

4. When did this happen? _____

5. Why do you think the students were quiet? _____

_____

_____

_____

_____

_____

_____

_____

_____

A or An

Use **a** before words that begin with a consonant sound. Use **an** before words that begin with a vowel sound.

> a cat   an egg

> Write a or an before each picture.

a n octopus

_____ snake

_____ zebra

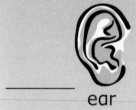
_____ ear

_____ telephone

_____ egg

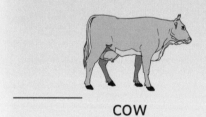
_____ cow

_____ umbrella

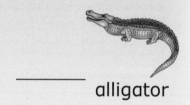
_____ alligator

_____ bear

_____ ant

_____ pig

A or An

Write a or an before each picture.

_____ elephant

_____ fox

_____ feather

_____ skunk

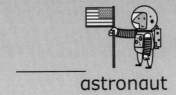
_____ astronaut

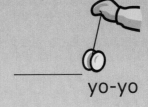
_____ yo-yo

_____ cone

_____ cup

_____ football

_____ cake

_____ flower

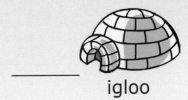
_____ igloo

A or An

Use **a** before words that begin with a consonant sound. Use **an** before words that begin with a vowel sound.

a cat   an egg

_____ goat

_____ gorilla

_____ dog

_____ sheep

_____ airplane

_____ apple

_____ envelope

_____ key

_____ cat

_____ arm

_____ hat

_____ bike

A or An

Read each sentence and circle the correct word.

1.   Sam hit   a - an   grand slam.

2.   Sam caught   a - an   fly ball.

3.   Sam made   a - an   homerun.

4.   Sam made   a - an   error on first base.

5.   Sam made   a - an   out.

6.   Sam made   a - an   base hit.

7.   Sam had   a - an   great game.

8.   Sam had   a - an   pizza after the game.

A or An

Use **a** before words that begin with a consonant sound. Use **an** before words that begin with a vowel sound.

Write a sentence about each picture.
Use a or an in each sentence.

1. _Rylie ate an apple._ _____

   _____

2. _____

   _____

3. _____

   _____

4. _____

   _____

5. _____

   _____

6. _____

   _____

A or An

1. He ate **a - an** apple.

2. He ate **a - an** sandwich.

3. He drank **a - an** orange soda.

4. He ate **a - an** hot dog.

5. He ate **a - an** egg.

6. He ate **a - an** candy bar.

7. He ate **a - an** ice cream cone.

8. He drank **a - an** glass of milk.

A or An

Use **a** before words that begin with a consonant sound. Use **an** before words that begin with a vowel sound.

> Write a sentence about each picture.
> Use a or an in each sentence.

1. _____
   _____

2. _____
   _____

3. _____
   _____

4. _____
   _____

5. _____
   _____

Alliteration

Alliteration is using the same letter or sounds at the beginning of words or syllables.

> Grady Grayson grew green grapes.

> Read these tongue-twisters aloud.

1. Clean clams crammed in clean cans

2. Tie twine to three tree twigs.

3. Six slimy snails sailed silently south.

4. Two tiny tigers took two taxis to town.

5. Rugged rubber baby bugger bumpers

> Underline the alliteration in each sentence.

7 1. Each Easter, Eddie eats eighty Easter eggs.

4 2. Goats gathered and gorged on grain.

4 3. Twelve twins twirled and twinkled.

6 4. Sister Susie sat sewing seven suits.

5 5. Betty Botter bought some bitter butter.

3 6. The witches wore watches.

7 7. A big black bug bit a big black bear.

Alliteration

Alliteration is using the same letter or sounds at the beginning of words or syllables.

> Use alliteration to finish the sentences.

1. Five filthy fellows _____

   _____

   _____

2. Really red robins _____

   _____

   _____

3. Big Ben bought _____

   _____

   _____

4. _____

   _____

   _____ dogs digging dirt.

5. _____

   _____

   _____ waded in the water.

Alliteration

Write a sentence about each picture using alliteration.

1. _____

_____

_____

2. _____

_____

_____

3. _____

_____

_____

4. _____

_____

_____

Rhymes & Riddles

Rhymes are words with the same ending sounds.

Write a rhyming word that answers each riddle.

1. I am something you wear on your finger.
   My name rhymes with swing.

   I am a ___ ___ ___ _g_.

2. I am something that you catch.
   My name rhymes with tall.

   I am a ___ ___ ___ ___.

3. I am something sweet to eat.
   My name rhymes with lake.

   I am a ___ ___ ___ ___.

4. I am something you sleep on.
   My name rhymes with red.

   I am a ___ ___ ___.

5. I am something that flies.
   My name rhymes with rat.

   I am a ___ ___ ___.

Rhymes & Riddles

A riddle is a puzzle in the form of a rhyme or question.

Answer each riddle and draw a line to the picture clue.

I'm a tasty fruit,
And I rhyme with glum;
And once I was stuck,
To Jack Horner's thumb.

What am I? ____ ____ ____ ____

A fruit of red or green,
And I start with a G;
My juice may be purple and sweet.
You can eat bunches of me.

What am I? ____ ____ ____ ____ ____

I can be a sour fruit,
And I start with C;
On top of whipped cream,
I make a yummy treat.

What am I? ____ ____ ____ ____ ____ ____

I'm a fuzzy, sweet fruit,
And I start with a P;
A pit is what is left,
When you're done eating me.

What am I? ____ ____ ____ ____ ____

Write each answer from above, then
write a word below it that rhymes.

_____   _____   _____   _____

_____   _____   _____   _____

Rhymes & Riddles

Fill in the chart using <u>Y</u> for yes and
<u>N</u> for no as you solve the puzzle.

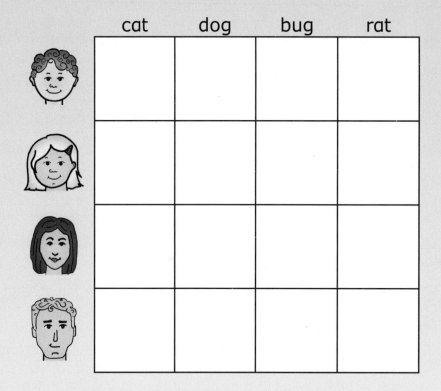

	cat	dog	bug	rat

Find each person's pet.

1. The names of the woman's pet and the boy's pet rhyme.

    _____   _____

2. The name of the man's pet rhymes with "jug."

    _____

3. The name of the woman's pet rhymes with "bat," "hat," and "cat."

    _____

Rhymes & Riddles

Fill in the chart using <u>Y</u> for yes and <u>N</u> for no as you solve the puzzle.

	yellow	red	black	silver
Aki				
Jack				
Dad				
Mom				

Each family member has a different favorite color. Figure out each person's favorite color.

1. Jack likes the color that rhymes with his name.

   _____

2. Jack's dad likes a color that rhymes with "fellow."

   _____

3. Aki's favorite color rhymes with "bed."

   _____

Rhymes & Riddles

Answer each riddle and draw a line to the picture clue. Then complete the picture clue.

I will be your friend,
And I start with d;
I will guard your house,
And I end with g.

What am I?   __ __ __

I will chase a mouse,
And I start with c;
I will chase a bird
And I end with t.

What am I?   __ __ __

I just love the mud,
And I start with p;
I am fat and smart,
And I end with g.

What am I?   __ __ __

Write each answer from above, then write a word below it that rhymes.

_____   _____   _____

_____   _____   _____

Rhymes & Riddles

Answer each riddle and draw a line to the picture clue. Then complete the picture clue.

As a baby, I'm called a cub.
Guess me, if you dare.
When I am grown,

You call me a __ _e_ __ __.

As a baby, I'm called a pup.
You can guess me, for real.
When I am grown,

You call me a __ __ _a_ __.

As a baby, I am called
A tadpole or polliwog.
But, when I am grown,

You call me a __ __ _o_ __.

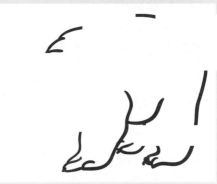

Write each answer from above, then write a word below it that rhymes.

_____   _____   _____

_____   _____   _____

Rhymes & Riddles

Answer each riddle.

As a baby, I'm called a kid.
I make milk for you to drink.
You can guess, just think.

What am I? __ o __ __

I will steal your cheese.
You don't want me in your house.

What am I? __ o u __ __ .

As a baby, I'm called a fawn or yearling.
I pull Santa's sleigh.
You can guess, do it today.

What am I?
__ e i __ __ e __ __

As a baby, I'm called a calf.
I start with w and end with e.
I am the largest animal in the sea.

What am I? __ __ __ __ __

I carry my home on my back.
I move very slow.
You can guess, I'm sure you know.

What am I?

__ u __ __ __ e

I start with s.
I end with e.
Don't always be afraid of me.

What am I?

__ __ __ k __

I start with c and end with e.
I live in water and on land.
Guess me, if you can.

What am I?

__ __ o __ o __ i __ __

I fly at night and hunt insects.
I can fly very far.
I don't see, but I have radar.

What am I?   __ __ __

Rhymes & Riddles

As a baby, I am called an eaglet.
I am the national bird.
You can guess me, it's an easy word.

What am I? __ __ __ __ e

As a baby, I'm called a bunny or kit.
I like to eat grass and hop very fast.
You can guess me, that is your task.

What am I?

__ a __ __ i __

My shell is round and hard.
Pearls are found inside of me.
You can find me in the sea.

What am I?

o __ __ __ __ __

My neck and legs are very long.
Guess me, you can't go wrong.

What am I?

__ i __ __ f __ e

I wear a white mask.
You may see me,
By the light of the moon.

What am I?

__ a __ __ o o __

I get fat by eating cheese.
Can you guess me, please?

What am I? __ a __

As a baby, I'm called a foal.
You can guess me, of course.

What am I? __ o __ __ e

Rhymes & Riddles

Answer each riddle.

As a baby, I'm called a cub or whelp.
You can guess me, you don't need help.

What am I? __ i __ e r

As a baby, I'm called a fry.
Guess me if you wish.
When I am grown,

What am I? __ i __ h

I eat lots of grass,
And I start with c;
The milk in your lunch,
All began with me.

What am I? __ __ __

As a baby, I'm called poult.
The sound I make is
gobble-gobble-gobble.
You may find me
on your Thanksgiving table.

What am I?

__ u __ __ __ y

I was huge.
I lived long ago.
You can guess, don't you know?

What am I?

__ i __ __ __ a u __

With two humps on my back,
I always have water to spare.
Guess me, if you dare.

What am I? __ a __ e __

Rhymes & Riddles

Read each line carefully and try to figure out what is being described.

I ride on water,
And I start with B;
With sail or motor,
You can go with me.

What am I? ___ ___ ___ ___

I start with an S,
And end with P;
And sail upon,
The salty sea.

What am I? ___ ___ ___ ___

To the dump I haul,
The garbage of the city;
And I rhyme with duck,
I hope you like this ditty.

What am I? ___ ___ ___ ___ ___

I have two wheels,
And I start with B;
Unless I'm training,
Then see four on me.

What am I? ___ ___ ___ ___ ___ ___ ___

Name four other types of transportation.

_____ _____ _____ _____

Rhymes & Riddles

Read each line carefully and try to figure out what is being described.

The color of the sky,
And I start with B;
And if it's deep and clear,
The lake is colored me.

What am I? ___ ___ ___ ___

The color of the sun,
And I start with Y;
There are two L's in me,
Guess me, oh please try.

What am I? ___ ___ ___ ___ ___ ___

The color of a juice,
And I end with E;
A fruit that is quite sweet,
Is named for me.

What am I? ___ ___ ___ ___ ___ ___

The color of a tree,
And I start with a G;
And if you have a lawn,
Let's hope it's colored me.

What am I? ___ ___ ___ ___ ___

Name four other colors.

_____   _____   _____   _____

Editor in Chief ®

Underline the alliteration in each story. Then circle the errors and write the corrections above the errors.

A Friend Indeed

15 alliteration, 2 subject-verb agreement, 2 spelling

One day, a little girl walked deep into the forest. She got tired of walking and decided to rest under a tree. Just then, forty fat frogs came hopping through the woods.

"Where are you going?" the little girl asked the frogs.

"We is going to town," one of the frogs answered, "where we will wander with a dozen dirty dogs."

As soon as the frogs left, a horse happened buy. When the little girl saw it, she cried, "Oh, won't you please give me a ride?"

The horse saw how tired the little girl was, so it agreed. The little girl climbed up on the horse and road it home. And forever after, the horse and the little girl was fast friends.

Homophones

Homophones are words that are spelled differently but sound the same.

Homophones

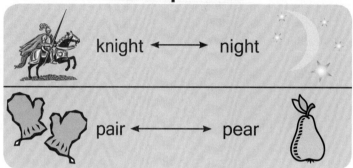

knight ←→ night

pair ←→ pear

Circle the correct homophone.

1. The boat sailed over the **see - (sea)**.

2. The crowd will come to **hear - here** the band.

3. The **ants - aunts** were crawling on the picnic table.

4. I went to the zoo and saw a **bare - bear**.

5. The house is over **their - there**.

6. The moon is over **their - there** house.

7. Those **rays - raise** from the sun are warm.

8. Please **pore - pour** me some milk.

9. My throat is **sore - soar**.

10. Please bring me a **pale - pail** of water.

11. I **mite - might** want to go.

12. Please stay out of **site - sight**.

Homophones

Complete each word and draw a line
to the picture that shows its meaning.

__ a i r   k __ i g h t   __ i g h t   __ e a r

Read the poem and answer the questions.

Pairs or Pears

Twelve pairs hanging high,
Twelve knights riding by,
Each knight took a pear,
And yet left a dozen there.

"Twelve pairs" means twelve sets of two. How many are twelve

sets of two? _____

How many knights took a pear? _____

How many are in a dozen? _____

Circle the picture that shows the correct ending to the poem.

Homophones

Homophones are words that are spelled differently but sound the same.

Homophones

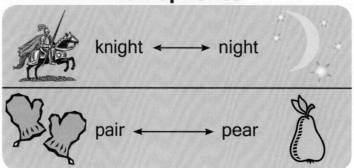

knight ⟷ night

pair ⟷ pear

Fill in each blank with a homophone from the choice box.

meat, meet; not, knot; our, hour; pail, pale; pain, pane; pair, pear; road, rode; sail, sale; bare, bear; see, sea; so, sew; sun, son; tail, tale; seller, cellar

1. Please come to __o__ __u__ __r__ house.

2. My cat's ___ ___ ___ ___ is white.

3. His ___ ___ ___ went home.

4. We had a ___ ___ ___ ___ for a snack.

5. I'll ___ ___ ___ ___ you after school.

6. The ship was lost at ___ ___ ___.

7. We had a ___ ___ ___ ___ of rabbits.

8. My mother went to a garage ___ ___ ___ ___.

9. Bob told a tall ___ ___ ___ ___.

10. The ___ ___ ___ was very bright.

11.   That ___ ___ ___ ___ went by fast.

12.   We had ___ ___ ___ ___ and vegetables for dinner.

13.   We walked down the ___ ___ ___ ___.

14.   The window ___ ___ ___ ___ is broken.

15.   That ___ ___ ___ ___ was hard to untie.

16.   He ___ ___ ___ ___ his bike to school.

17.   Carl carried a ___ ___ ___ ___ of water.

18.   Sue has a ___ ___ ___ ___ in her leg.

19.   Mike has a ___ ___ ___ ___ boat.

20.   We saw a ___ ___ ___ ___ at the zoo.

21.   That color is too ___ ___ ___ ___.

22.   I do ___ ___ ___ want to go.

23.   I ___ ___ ___ the birds in the nest.

24.   My feet are ___ ___ ___ ___.

25.   We went down to the ___ ___ ___ ___ ___ ___.

26.   John was the ___ ___ ___ ___ ___ ___ of the car.

Homophones

Homophones are words that are spelled differently but sound the same.

Homophones

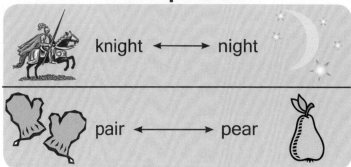

knight ⟵⟶ night

pair ⟵⟶ pear

Fill in each blank with a homophone from the choice box.

ant, aunt; nose, knows; deer, dear; eight, ate; hair, hare; for, four; caller, collar; eye, I; here, hear; blue, blew; made, maid; bee, be; cent, scent; beet, beat

1. __I__ have a black dog.

2. Mary ___ ___ ___ all the cookies.

3. The ___ ___ ___ ___ ran across the road.

4. The ___ ___ ___ stung me.

5. ___ ___ ___ ___ I am.

6. Tim ___ ___ ___ ___ his bed.

7. My ___ ___ ___ ___ visited us today.

8. The wind ___ ___ ___ ___ really hard.

9. He had a patch over one ___ ___ ___.

10. She ___ ___ ___ ___ ___ the rules of the game.

11. Sue's ___ ___ ___ ___ is red.

12. Her ___ ___ ___ ___ ___ ___ kept her neck warm.

13. The piece of gum cost one ___ ___ ___ ___.

14. Mike will ___ ___ there soon.

15. There were ___ ___ ___ ___ ___ puppies.

16. The flower had a pretty ___ ___ ___ ___ ___.

17. Did you ___ ___ ___ ___ from your sister?

18. They have a ___ ___ ___ ___ to clean the bedrooms.

19. The ___ ___ ___ followed the sugar trail.

20. A ___ ___ ___ ___ has longer ears than a rabbit.

21. He had a runny ___ ___ ___ ___.

22. The sky is ___ ___ ___ ___.

23. The ___ ___ ___ ___ ___ ___ wanted to talk to Jim.

24. You begin a letter with "___ ___ ___ ___."

25. We voted ___ ___ ___ Mike.

26. My brother is ___ ___ ___ ___ years old.

Homographs

Homographs are words that are spelled the same but sound different.

Homographs

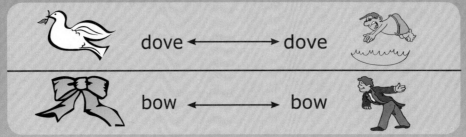

Read each sentence and fill in the correct homograph.

~~lead~~   presents   polish   tear   close   live

1. L e a d me to a pencil that has l e a d .

2. We need to buy __ __ __ __ __ __ sausage and shoe

    __ __ __ __ __ __ __.

3. Is there a __ __ __ __ in your eye because of the

    __ __ __ __ in your shirt?

4. I am __ __ __ __ __ to the door so I will

    __ __ __ __ __ it.

5. __ __ __ __ animals __ __ __ __ at the zoo.

6. My mom __ __ __ __ __ __ __ __ __ my

    __ __ __ __ __ __ __ __ to me on my birthday.

Homographs

Read each sentence and fill in the correct homograph.

b~~ass~~   wind   minute   desert   lead   bow

1. He likes to fish for _bass_ and play the _bass_ guitar.

2. The center black part of your pencil is ___ ___ ___ ___.

3. A guide dog can ___ ___ ___ ___ a blind person.

4. The ___ ___ ___ ___ blew the door open.

5. Don't forget to ___ ___ ___ ___ the clock.

6. I will not ___ ___ ___ ___ ___ ___ my friends in the

   ___ ___ ___ ___ ___ ___.

7. We cannot see germs because they are so

   ___ ___ ___ ___ ___ ___.

8. Sixty seconds equals one ___ ___ ___ ___ ___ ___ .

9. She has a beautiful ___ ___ ___ in her hair.

10. The dancers will ___ ___ ___ to the audience.

Homographs

Homographs are words that are spelled the same but sound different.

Use the <u>code</u> to find the vowels to complete the homographs. Write the word and then write two sentences, one for each meaning.

t [a] [a] r   _t e a r_

_____ He had a tear in his eye. _____

_____ He had a tear in his pants. _____

d [o] v [e]   _ _ _ _ _

_____

_____

w [i] n d   _ _ _ _ _

_____

_____

b ▽ w _ _ _

_____

_____

pr □ s □ n t s _____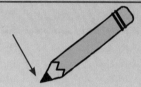

_____

_____

l □ ◣ d _ _ _ _

_____

_____

d □ s □ r t _____

_____

_____

Multiple Meaning Words

Multiple meaning words* are words that have more than one meaning, depending on how they are used in a sentence.

Used as a noun

The bat flew through the night sky.

Used as a verb

Marcia is going to bat the ball.

Write the word from the choice box that completes both sentences.

pet   name   ~~cover~~   check   paint   play   trip

1. Put the c o v e r on the box.

   Please c o v e r the meat so it won't spoil.

2. The cat is my favorite ___ ___ ___.

   I like to sit and ___ ___ ___ my cat.

3. The artist will ___ ___ ___ ___ ___ another picture.

   I accidentally sat in some wet ___ ___ ___ ___ ___.

4. My family will take a ___ ___ ___ ___ to the lake this summer.

   If you don't watch where you're walking, you might ___ ___ ___ ___.

5. My little brother likes to ___ ___ ___ ___ with his blocks.

   I went to see the ___ ___ ___ ___ with my parents.

6. Please ___ ___ ___ ___ ___ to make sure we have enough milk.

   My grandmother gave me a ___ ___ ___ ___ ___ for my birthday.

7. Please tell me your ___ ___ ___ ___ and address.

   I am going to ___ ___ ___ ___ my dog Rufus.

*Note to Teacher: Homographs are multiple meaning words.

Multiple Meaning Words

Write the noun from the choice box that completes the sentence. Then write another sentence using the word as a verb.

~~cut~~   color   wish   tire   walk   shape

1. I have a paper <u>C</u> <u>U</u> <u>t</u> on my hand and it hurts!

   <u>My mom used a knife to cut the cake.</u>

   _____

2. Make a ___ ___ ___ ___ and blow out the candles.

   _____

   _____

3. A triangle is a ___ ___ ___ ___ ___.

   _____

   _____

4. I'm going to take a ___ ___ ___ ___ through the park.

   _____

   _____

5. Green is my favorite ___ ___ ___ ___ ___.

   _____

   _____

6. Dad bought a spare ___ ___ ___ ___ for the car.

   _____

   _____

Me & I

When you talk or write about someone else and yourself, name yourself last.

Me	**I**

Use <u>me</u> when the subject is doing something to or with you.

 Bob is throwing to <u>me</u>.

Bob is playing catch with <u>me</u>.

Use <u>I</u> when you are part of the subject.

 Bob and <u>I</u> are playing catch.

Read each sentence and circle the correct word.

1. Joey and **me - I** are friends.
2. He and **me - I** are like brothers.
3. He likes to talk to **me - I** on the phone.
4. **Me - I** like to talk to him on the phone.
5. He likes to play with **me - I**.
6. He and **me - I** like to play soccer.
7. Sometimes **me - I** like to go to his house.
8. Sometimes he wants to come to see **me - I**.
9. He and **me - I** both like to play soccer.
10. **Me - I** like to read to him.

Write one sentence about your best friend using <u>me</u>. Write another sentence about your best friend using <u>I</u>.

<u>Me</u> sentence: _____

_____

<u>I</u> sentence: _____

_____

Me & I

Read each sentence and circle the correct word.

1. Joy and me - I are friends.

2. She and me - I are like sisters.

3. She likes to play with me - I.

4. She and me - I like to fish.

5. Sometimes me - I like to go to her house.

6. Sometimes she wants to come to see me - I.

7. She and me - I both like to read.

8. Me - I like to read to her.

9. She likes to read to me - I.

10. She likes to call me - I on the phone.

Write one sentence about another friend using <u>me</u>.
Then write another sentence about that friend using <u>I</u>.

<u>Me</u> sentence: _____

_____

<u>I</u> sentence: _____

_____

Was & Were

The verbs **was** and **were** tell about someone or something in the past.

Was

Use was with one person, place, or thing.

Our home was cold.

The car was cold.

Use was with the word I.

Last night I was cold.

Were

Use were with more than one person, place, or thing.

We were cold.

The houses were cold.

Use were with the word you.

You were cold.

Complete each sentence with was or were.

Yesterday, the dogs _____ eating.

Yesterday, I _____ feeding the dog.

Yesterday, the girl _____ feeding the dogs.

Yesterday, the girls _____ feeding the dogs.

Was & Were

 Yesterday, the cat _____ eating.

  Yesterday, the cats

_____ eating.

 Yesterday, I _____ feeding the cat.

  Yesterday, the boys

_____ feeding

the cats.

Language Smarts™ Level C

Was & Were

The verbs **was** and **were** tell about someone or something in the past.

Was		**Were**	
Use was with one person, place, or thing.	Use was with the word I.	Use were with more than one person, place, or thing.	Use were with the word you.

The car was cold.
Our home was cold.

Last night I was cold.

The houses were cold.
We were cold.

You were cold.

> Complete each sentence below with <u>was</u> or <u>were</u>.

Yesterday, the clowns _____ giving the children a balloon.

Yesterday, the clown _____ giving the girl a balloon.

Yesterday, the children _____ getting a balloon from the clown.

Yesterday, I _____ giving the girl a balloon.

Was & Were

Read each sentence and circle the correct word.

1. Yesterday **was - were** my birthday.

2. I **was - were** eight years old.

3. I **was - were** very happy.

4. My family **was - were** at my party.

5. My friends **was - were** there.

6. My grandmother **was - were** there.

7. My cousins **was - were** there.

8. My cake **was - were** chocolate.

9. My balloons **was - were** red.

10. It **was - were** a great day.

Write one sentence about your birthday using was.
Write another sentence about your birthday using were.

_____

_____

_____

_____

Was & Were

The verbs **was** and **were** tell about someone or something in the past.

> Read each sentence and circle the correct word.

1. Yesterday was - were my first soccer game.

2. I was - were proud to be on the team.

3. I was - were very happy.

4. My family was - were at my game.

5. My friends was - were there.

6. My grandmother was - were there.

7. My cousins was - were there.

8. My uniform was - were red and white.

9. My hat was - were red.

10. It was - were a great day.

> Write one sentence about your favorite sport using <u>was</u>.
> Write another sentence about your favorite sport using <u>were</u>.

_____

_____

_____

_____

Editor in Chief®

In the fable, write was or were in the spaces. Then circle the spelling errors and write the correction above each error.

The Ant and the Chrysalis

4 was, 1 were, 2 spelling

Some ants _____ running about in search of food. One ant came across a chrysalis that _____ very near its time of change. The chrysalis moved its tale and attracted the attention of the ant, who then saw that it _____ alive.

"Poor animal!" cried the ant. "How sad! While I can run around at my pleasure, you lie here with the power only to move a joint or two of your tail."

The chrysalis herd all this but did not try to make any reply. A few days later, when the ant _____ passing that way again, nothing but the cocoon remained. Wondering what had become of its contents, the ant felt himself suddenly shaded and fanned by the wings of a beautiful butterfly. The butterfly said, "Boast now of your powers to run and climb."

Then, the butterfly rose in the air and _____ soon lost to the sight of the ant forever.

MORAL: Appearances are deceptive.

Writing Detective®

Read the story and then answer the questions based on the best evidence in the story.

Good Today and Better Tomorrow

[1]Bunny and Hedgehog had a picnic on Thursday. [2]They brought potato salad for Hedgehog and carrots for Bunny.

[3]"This is the best picnic we've ever had," Hedgehog said. [4]He helped himself to some more potato salad.

[5]"I'll say!" said Bunny, as he crunched and munched on another carrot. [6]"This is even better than yesterday!"

[7]"Far better," agreed Hedgehog. [8]"And I can't wait for tomorrow's picnic! [9]It will probably be even better!"

[10]"I'm sure tomorrow's picnic will be the best yet," Bunny said.

[11]"And, for a change, how about lettuce?"

[12]"Let us what?" asked Hedgehog.

[13]"No, not let us," Bunny said. [14]"I said lettuce."

[15]"Oh, phooey!" Hedgehog said. [16]"I'm going home now." [17]And with that, he scurried away.

Reading Questions

1. What sentences tell you what Hedgehog was eating? _____ _____

2. What sentence tells you they had a picnic the day before? _____

3. How often do you think they had picnics?

   _____

   What two sentences are the best evidence for your answer?

   _____ _____

4. Number the events from 1–5 in the order they happened in the story.

   ____ Hedgehog helped himself to some more potato salad.

   ____ Bunny suggested they have some lettuce.

   ____ Hedgehog scurried away.

   ____ Bunny munched on another carrot.

   ____ Hedgehog said tomorrow's picnic would be even better.

Now that you've read the story and answered the questions, write a paragraph about what the story was about. Before you write your paragraph, look at the questions and make some notes about the story to guide you when you write.

1. Who is the story about? _____

2. What were they doing? _____

3. Where did this happen? _____

4. When did this happen? _____

5. What words did Bunny and Hedgehog confuse? _____

_____

_____

_____

_____

_____

_____

_____

_____

_____

_____

Facts and Inferences

A story has two types of information: facts and inferences. **Facts** are clearly stated in the story. **Inferences** are conclusions you make about the story. They are based on information suggested in the story and sometimes on your own knowledge and experience.

> See if you can tell the difference between an inference and a fact in the following story.

New Snow

The sun sparkled on the new snow. Almost a foot had fallen since last night. Now the sky was clear. It was going to be a beautiful day. "A perfect day to be sledding," thought Jesse, as his bus pulled into the school parking lot.

> Find the two facts and two inferences. Write fact or inference after each statement.

There was new snow.   _____

Jesse is a student.   _____

The sky was clear.   _____

Jesse would rather be sledding.   _____

Facts and Inferences

See if you can tell the difference between an inference and a fact in the following story.

The Snowman

It snowed on Sunday, and Jill built a snowman. She put an old cap and two button eyes on its head. It looked wonderful! The next morning, the sun was shining. The snowman was still in the yard. When Jill got home from school, there were only a cap and two buttons on the ground.

Find the two facts and two inferences. Write fact or inference after each statement.

It snowed on Sunday.   _____

Jill was in school on Monday.   _____

Monday was a warm day.   _____

The snowman disappeared on Monday. _____

Facts and Inferences

A story has two types of information: facts and inferences. **Facts** are clearly stated in the story. **Inferences** are conclusions you make about the story. They are based on information suggested in the story and sometimes on your own knowledge and experience.

> See if you can tell the difference between an inference and a fact in the following story.

Lunch Time

Megan was sitting alone at the lunch table. As always, her nose was buried in a book. "Is anyone sitting here?" I asked. Megan didn't answer, so I sat down. "Must be a really good book," I said. Megan just sniffed and kept on reading. I tried again. "I like mysteries, too." This time, Megan glared at me, slammed the book shut, and left.

> Write fact or inference beside each statement.

Megan wants to be left alone.   _____

Megan was sitting alone.   _____

Megan slammed the book shut and left.   _____

Megan likes to read.   _____

Facts and Inferences

See if you can tell the difference between an inference and a fact in the following story.

Sarah's Birthday

Today is a special day. Sarah sees Grandpa coming up the stairs with a brightly colored package in his hands. Sarah thinks the box looks like the right size for a book. Sarah hopes Grandpa remembered what she wanted most for her birthday.

Write fact or inference beside each statement.

Sarah will get a book for her birthday.   _____

Grandpa was carrying a package.   _____

Today is a special day.   _____

Sarah likes to read.   _____

Fact or Opinion

A **fact** can be proved to be true.

A giraffe has a long neck.

An **opinion** is how you feel or what you think about something.

Peas taste terrible.

Read each sentence and circle if it is fact or opinion.

1. Red is the prettiest color.   Fact   (Opinion)

2. There are seven days in a week.   Fact   Opinion

3. Cows give milk.   Fact   Opinion

4. George Washington was president.   Fact   Opinion

5. Halloween is in October.   Fact   Opinion

6. There are 60 minutes in an hour.   Fact   Opinion

7. Pizza is the best food.   Fact   Opinion

8. A grape is smaller than a peach.   Fact   Opinion

9. Grapes taste better than peaches.   Fact   Opinion

10. Puppies are cuter than kittens.   Fact   Opinion

Fact or Opinion

Write a fact about each picture. Make sure your answer is a complete sentence.

1. ___Apples grow on trees.___

2. _____

3. _____

4. _____

Fact or Opinion

A **fact** can be proved to be true.
An **opinion** is how you feel or what you think about something.

Write an opinion about each picture. Make sure
your answer is a complete sentence.

1. *The boys had fun swimming in the lake.*

2. _____

3. _____

4. _____

Fact or Opinion

Write two sentences about each picture.
Make one a fact and the other an opinion.

1. _____

_____

_____

2. _____

_____

_____

3. _____

_____

_____

4. _____

_____

_____

Nonfiction and Fiction

Nonfiction
A true story about real things, people, events, and places.

↓

Real
Things and events that are or were part of our world.

Fiction
A story that is not true.

↓

Not Real
Things and events that never happened.

Read the stories and circle the correct answers.

Hunting Lions
Lions are predators. They are very fast runners, and they have very good vision. They chase and catch their prey. They like to feed on deer, zebras, rabbits, and squirrels.

The characters in this story are real - not real.

This story is fiction - nonfiction.

What character or event led you to your answer?

_____

Jan, the Lion Mom
Jan is a lion who lives with a group of lions in a pride. She sometimes scolds her cubs for going too far into the bush where she can't see them. She loves them, but they are a lot of work. Some days she wishes she could make them take a nap, so she could have a break.

The characters in this story are real - not real.

This story is fiction - nonfiction.

What character or event led you to your answer?

_____

Write a fiction and a nonfiction story.

Fiction:_____

_____

_____

_____

_____

_____

_____

Nonfiction: _____

_____

_____

_____

_____

_____

_____

_____

Nonfiction and Fiction

Nonfiction

A true story about real things, people, events, and places.

Fiction

A story that is not true.

Write your own nonfiction story about lions.

_____

_____

_____

_____

_____

_____

_____

_____

_____

_____

_____

_____

_____

Nonfiction and Fiction

Nonfiction

A true story about real things, people, events, and places.

Fiction

A story that is not true.

Fantasy

A fiction story involving magic and supernatural characters.

Real

Things and events that are or were part of our world.

Not Real

Things and events that never happened.

Nonfiction and Fiction

Nonfiction

A true story about real things, people, events, and places.

↓

Real

Things and events that are or were part of our world.

Fiction

A story that is not true.

↓

Fantasy

A fiction story involving magic and supernatural characters.

↓

Not Real

Things and events that never happened.

Read the poem and circle the correct answers.

The Wizard's Helper

The wizard left for the day,
Leaving chores for Mickey, who wanted to play.
He waved the wand to cast a spell,
The broom worked hard, carrying water from the well.
The wizard returned to find a mess.
Mickey hung his head and had to confess.

The characters and events in the poem are **real - not real.**

This story is **fiction, but not fantasy - fantasy.**

What character or event in the poem led to your answer?

_____

_____

Nonfiction and Fiction

Read the story and circle the correct answers.

Just the Ticket
Jimmy grabbed the envelope from the mailbox and ran into the house. "It's here!" he yelled to Sarah. He sat down at the table and was opening the envelope when his sister walked in. Jimmy held up the tickets. "We're going to the big game, Sarah!" he said, with a grin.

The characters and events in the story are real - not real.

This story is nonfiction - fantasy.

Hey, Diddle, Diddle!

Hey, Diddle, Diddle!
The cat and the fiddle,
The cow jumped over the moon;
The little dog laughed
To see such sport,
And the dish ran away with the spoon.

Circle the correct answers.

The characters and events in the poem are real - not real.

This story is fiction, but not fantasy - fantasy.

What character or event in the story led you to your answer?

_____

Nonfiction and Fiction

Fiction is a story that is not true.

Write a fiction story that is not a fantasy.

_____

_____

_____

_____

_____

Fantasy is a fiction story involving magic and supernatural characters.

Write a fantasy story.

_____

_____

_____

_____

_____

Nonfiction and Fiction

Nonfiction

A true story about real things, people, events, and places.

Fiction

A story that is not true.

Circle the correct answers.

A school report is nonfiction - fiction.

A letter to a friend describing your favorite food is nonfiction - fiction.

The directions to your house are nonfiction - fiction.

A make believe story about a normal dog is nonfiction - fiction.

An invitation to your friend's party is nonfiction - fiction.

A story about an imaginary mouse is nonfiction - fiction.

Nonfiction and Fiction

Read the story and circle the correct answers.

George Washington

George Washington is often called "the father of his country" for leading the United States of America in its earliest days. He was the country's first president.

GEORGE WASHINGTON
The 1st U.S. President
1789-1797

The characters and events in the story are **real - not real**.

This story is **nonfiction - fiction**.

Read the poem and circle the correct answers.

Itsy Bitsy Spider

The itsy bitsy spider
Climbed up the water spout;
Down came the rain
And washed the spider out;
Out came the sun
And dried up all the rain;
So the itsy bitsy spider
climbed up the spout again.

The characters and events in the poem are **real - not real**.

This poem is **fiction, but not fantasy - fantasy**.

What character or event in the poem led to your answer?

_____

_____

Poems

Poems that rhyme are called verse. Poems that do not rhyme are called prose.

Verse

Prose

Vital Question
By Gordon Korman

If a poem doesn't rhyme
How do you know
It's a poem?
If it's about sunsets and flowers, well okay.

But some of them might be about termites, and rats,
Cockroaches, earwigs, bedbugs,
And silverfish,
Battalions of cooties,
And are more like the exterminator's report
Than a poem.

So how do you know it's a poem
If it doesn't rhyme?

Is the poem verse or prose? _____

Write 1 or 2 sentences of prose about one of these pictures.

_____

_____

_____

_____

Poems

Poems that rhyme are called verse. Poems that do not rhyme are called prose.

Verse

Prose

April Rain Song
By Langston Hughes

Let the rain kiss you.
Let the rain beat upon your head with silver liquid drops.
Let the rain sing you a lullaby.
The rain makes still pools on the sidewalk.
The rain makes running pools in the gutter.
The rain plays a little sleep-song on our roof at night—
And I love the rain.

Is the poem verse or prose? _____

Write 1 or 2 sentences of prose about one of these pictures.

_____

_____

_____

_____

Poems

The Fly
By Ogden Nash

[1]The Lord in His wisdom made the fly
[2]And then forgot to tell us why.

Which words rhyme? _____ _____

Is this poem verse or prose? _____

Write 1 or 2 sentences of verse about one of these pictures.

_____

_____

_____

_____

_____

Poems

Poems that rhyme are called verse. Poems that do not rhyme are called prose.

Draw a line to connect the words that rhyme.

My Nose
By Dorothy Aldis

[1]It doesn't breathe;

[2]It doesn't smell;

[3]It doesn't feel

[4]So very well.

[5]I am discouraged

[6]With my nose:

[7]The only thing it

[8]Does is blows.

Write the number of the lines that rhyme.

_____ and _____   _____ and _____

Write 1 or 2 sentences of verse about one of these pictures.

_____

_____

_____

Folktales

Folktales are stories that have been passed down for many years. Before books, TV, movies, and videos were invented, people often learned information through stories.

Folktales

Fairy Tale

Fable

A story about things that we want or things that we are afraid of. They usually have a fairy godmother or another supernatural character. They usually have happy endings.

A story about animals that think, speak, and act like people. They usually teach important lessons.

Answer the following questions

1. Is a fairy tale a folktale? _____

2. Is a fable a folktale? _____

3. Is a fable a fairy tale? _____

4. Is a fairy tale a fable? _____

Folktales

Folk Tales

Fairy Tale  Fable

A story about things that we want or things that we are afraid of. They usually have a fairy godmother or another supernatural character. They usually have happy endings.

A story about animals that think, speak, and act like people. They usually teach important lessons.

Read the story and circle the correct answer.

The Dog and the Shadow

Grandpa is telling a story about a dog carrying a piece of meat. As he was crossing a creek, the dog looked down and saw his shadow. He thought it was another dog with meat and tried to grab it. When he opened his mouth, the meat fell into the creek. He went home with nothing to eat.

Grandpa is telling a fairy tale - fable.

Folktales

Read the story and circle the correct answer.

The Turtle and the Rabbit

Grandpa is telling a story about a turtle and a rabbit that are in a race. The rabbit thought he could beat the turtle, so he took a nap. The turtle moved slow and steady. He won the race!

Grandpa is telling a fairy tale - fable.

Read the story and circle the correct answer.

The Poisoned Apple

Grandpa is telling a story about a beautiful girl who ate a poisoned apple. A mean witch was jealous of the beautiful girl and wanted to get rid of her. Finally, after sleeping for a long time, a handsome prince kissed her and she woke up. They all lived happily ever after.

Grandpa is telling a fairy tale - fable.

Folktales

Fairy Tale

A story about things that we want or things that we are afraid of. They usually have a fairy godmother or another supernatural character. They usually have happy endings.

Complete the titles of the fairy tales below.

___ ___ ___ d e r e l l ___

___ a c k **and the**
___ ___ a n s t a l k

___ n o w
___ h i t e **and the**
S e v ___ ___
___ ___ a ___ v ___ ___

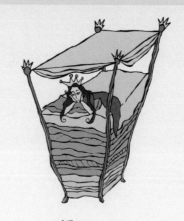

___ I ___ ___
P r i n c e ___ ___
and the ___ e a

Folktales

Fable

A story about animals that think, speak, and act like people. They usually teach important lessons.

Complete the titles of the fables below.

_ i t t l e
_ _ _
Riding Hood

_ _ _   _ h r e e
_ _ _ _ _
Pigs

_ _ _ e
_ o r t o i s e
and the Hare

Goldilocks _ _ _
the _ _ _ _ _
Bears

Folktales

Fairy Tale

A story about things that we want or things that we are afraid of. They usually have a fairy godmother or another supernatural character. They usually have happy endings.

Fable

A story about animals that think, speak, and act like people. They usually teach important lessons.

Read the story and circle the correct answers.

The Ant and the Dove

An ant went to the bank of a river to get a drink of water. He was swept away by the rush of the stream. The ant was beginning to drown when a dove, sitting on a tree that was overhanging the water, plucked a leaf and let it fall into the stream close to her. The ant climbed onto it and floated safely to the bank.

Shortly afterwards a bird catcher came and stood under the tree and laid a trap for the dove, which sat in the branches. The ant saw the trap and stung the bird catcher on the foot. In pain, the bird catcher threw down the twigs, and the noise made the dove fly away.

1. This story is a **fable - fairy tale**.

2. The theme of this story is:

   a. Do unto others as you would have them do unto you.

   b. Little by little does the trick.

   c. It is best to plan ahead.

Folktales

Read the story and circle the correct answers.

The Crow and the Pitcher

A crow was very thirsty. He saw a pitcher and flew down to drink from it. When he reached it, he discovered that it contained so little water that he could not possibly get to it. He tried and he tried, but at last he had to give up. Then a thought came to him. He took a pebble and dropped it into the pitcher. Then he repeated this several more times. At last, he saw the water rise up near him, and after dropping in a few more pebbles, he was able to quench his thirst.

1. This story is a fable - fairy tale.

2. The theme of this story is:

   a. Do unto others as you would have them do unto you.

   b. Little by little does the trick.

   c. It is best to plan ahead.

Folktales

Fairy Tale

A story about things that we want or things that we are afraid of. They usually have a fairy godmother or another supernatural character. They usually have happy endings.

Fable

A story about animals that think, speak, and act like people. They usually teach important lessons.

Write your favorite folktale. It can be a fairy tale or a fable.

_____

_____

_____

_____

_____

_____

_____

_____

What is the name of your folktale?

_____

Is your folktale a fairy tale or a fable? _____

Folktales

Draw a picture of your favorite folktale. It can be a fairy tale or a fable. Then answer the questions.

What is the name of your folktale?

_____

Is your folk tale a fairy tale or a fable? _____

Setting

The **setting** is the time and place in which a story takes place. Sometimes you are told the exact time and place. Other times, there may be clues that suggest when and where the story happens.

The Green House

As they stood inside, they could look down on the whole neighborhood. They pulled up the rope ladder so no one would know they were up there. It was Saturday morning. Mrs. Perkins was hanging her wash. Mr. Fuji was washing his car. No one could see them hidden up there in the tree's leafy branches.

When did the story take place? Write a complete sentence.

_____

_____

Where did the story take place? Write a complete sentence.

_____

_____

Setting

The **setting** is the time and place in which a story takes place. Sometimes you are told the exact time and place. Other times, there may be clues that suggest when and where the story happens.

The Bird

It was Saturday morning. Billy was playing in his backyard when he heard a loud tap-tap-tap. The noise was coming from a tree in his yard, but no one was in the tree. There was only a bird with a pointed beak.

When did the story take place? Write a complete sentence.

_____

_____

Where did the story take place? Write a complete sentence.

_____

_____

Characters

You learn what a **character** is like as you read what he or she does and says. A character's words and actions tell you what kind of person he or she is. A character may be kind or mean, silly or serious, or brave or timid.

Mrs. Chan's Desk

"Has anyone seen my new pen?" asked Mrs. Chan. "I know it was right here a minute ago." As I looked at her desk, there wasn't an empty space anywhere. Some piles were a foot deep. Mrs. Chan never got rid of anything. The last time I helped her look for something, we found an old piece of birthday cake in her desk.

Circle every word that would describe Mrs. Chan.

1. funny

2. messy

3. tidy

4. strict

Characters

The Bus Line

Arthur wants to be first in line. When the bell rings, he runs as fast as he can to line up. Once, he knocked Taima to the ground but kept going. When Kiri gets there before him, he tries to push her out of line.

In the story, what is the character like? Write a complete sentence.

_____

_____

What do you think would happen if Arthur's teacher told everyone to get on the bus? Write complete sentences.

_____

_____

_____

Conflict

A **conflict** is the main problem in the story. There may be a conflict between one character and another. Sometimes the conflict is between a character and something else, such as nature. A character can even have an inner conflict when he or she isn't sure what to do.

Alone In the Woods

It was getting darker and colder. He stumbled through the brush. Thorny branches scratched him and tore at his clothes. He jumped when he heard a rustling in the bushes. He was thirsty, but he no longer knew where the river was. Soon he wouldn't be able to see anything. Would anyone come to find him?

Circle the sentence that best describes the conflict in the story.

1. The conflict is between the boy and nature.

2. The conflict is between the boy and himself.

3. The conflict is between the boy and his best friend.

Conflict

The Bird's Nest

Aaron liked to climb trees. One day, he found a bird nest in a tall tree. Inside the nest were five blue eggs. Aaron wanted to take one egg back to show his brother, but he knew that he should not take the egg from the nest. Finally, Aaron decided to leave the eggs in the nest.

Circle the sentence that best describes the conflict in the story.

1. The conflict is between the boy and nature.

2. The conflict is between the boy and himself.

3. The conflict is between the boy and his best friend.

Conflict

A **conflict** is the main problem in the story. There may be a conflict between one character and another. Sometimes the conflict is between a character and something else, such as nature. A character can even have an inner conflict when he or she isn't sure what to do.

Saturday Mornings

On Saturday mornings, Jesse and his sister, Megan, liked to eat breakfast while they watched TV. Last Saturday morning, Jesse wanted to watch channel 5 and his sister wanted to watch channel 10. They could not agree on which channel to watch.

What is the conflict in the story? Circle the best answer.

1. The conflict is between the boy and the TV.

2. The conflict is between the boy and himself.

3. The conflict is between the boy and his sister.

Topic and Main Idea

Stories have a **topic** and a **main idea**. The topic tells you what the story is about. The main idea tells you what the author wants to say about the topic.

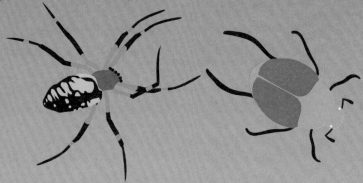

Spiders and Insects

There are many differences between spiders and insects. A spider's body has two main parts. An insect's body has three main parts. A spider has eight legs. An insect has six legs. Most insects have wings and spiders don't. An insect has antennae and spiders don't.

Circle the topic of the story.

1. Spiders

2. Insects

3. Spiders and insects

4. Spiders and people

Circle the main idea of the story.

1. Similarities between spiders and insects

2. Scary spiders and insects

3. What spiders and insects eat

4. Differences between spiders and insects

Topic and Main Idea

Stories have a **topic** and a **main idea**. The topic tells you what the story is about. The main idea tells you what the author wants to say about the topic.

Butterflies

Butterflies are insects. Butterflies have three main body parts. Insects have three main body parts. Butterflies have six legs. Insects have six legs. Butterflies have antennae. Insects have antennae.

Circle the topic of the story.

1. Insects
2. Butterflies
3. Three body parts
4. Legs

Circle the main idea of the story.

1. Butterflies have three body parts.
2. Insects have antennae.
3. Insects have six legs.
4. Butterflies are insects.

Topic and Main Idea

Ladybugs

Ladybugs are insects. They have six legs and antennae. Insects also have six legs and antennae. The ladybug has big wings that are covered by a hard outer shell. Ladybugs are helpers in the garden because they eat other insects that chew on plant leaves.

Circle the topic of the story.

1. Insects
2. Ladybugs
3. Legs
4. Antennae

Circle the main idea of the story.

1. Ladybugs have six legs.
2. Insects have three main body parts.
3. Ladybugs have three main body parts.
4. Ladybugs are insects.

Theme

The **theme** of a story is the human meaning behind the events, such as friendship, honesty, or courage.

The Ball Game

Beni loves to watch baseball. He spent all his money on his ticket to the game. Now the game is over.

As he leaves the ball park, he finds a wallet on the ground. It has $10 in it. That's enough to get a ticket to another game. He could keep the money and leave the wallet. But that wallet and money belong to someone else. He looks inside the wallet and finds its owner's name.

"Oliver! Oliver Randall!" he shouts. Oliver Randall was leaving but comes back when he hears his name.

Oliver is surprised to see his lost wallet. "I'm so happy to get it back. Thank you for being honest."

Beni left the ball park feeling good about doing the right thing.

Circle the best theme for this story.

1. Ball games are fun.

2. Being brave is important.

3. Honesty is its own reward.

Theme

Gina and Her Brother

   Gina was walking with her little brother down a sidewalk when a group of boys on bikes came racing up behind them. The boys were racing and approached at reckless speed. Gina was frightened, but she knew she had to act quickly. She jumped in front of her little brother and wrapped her arms around him to protect him from the speeding bikes. The boys were gone in a flash. Gina's heart was pounding. Her little brother was frightened and crying, but most importantly, he was safe.

Circle the best theme of the story.

1. Honesty is always best.

2. It isn't always easy to be brave.

3. Friendships can take time.

Alternative Endings

An **alternative ending** is when a story ends in a different way.

Read the first fable with its familiar ending.

The Lion and The Mouse

A lion was taking a nap one day when a little mouse ran over his face. The lion grabbed the little mouse by its tail and said, "You woke me up! Just for that, I'm going to eat you!"

"Please don't kill me, Mr. Lion!" the mouse cried. "If you let me go, maybe I'll be able to do something for you someday."

That made the lion laugh. "You? Do something for me? That's a joke!" But he was amused by the little mouse, so he let him go.

The next day, the lion got caught in a trap. The hunters tied the lion to a tree while they went to get a cart to carry him away. The lion roared and the little mouse heard him. He realized the lion was in trouble and he needed to try to help him. When the little mouse saw the lion was tied with a rope, he scampered over and began to gnaw at the rope. Soon, the lion was free.

Now read the fable with an alternative ending.

The Lion and The Mouse

A lion was taking a nap one day when a little mouse ran over its face. The lion grabbed the little mouse by its tail and said, "You woke me up! Just for that, I'm going to eat you!"

"Please don't kill me, Mr. Lion!" the mouse cried. "If you let me go, maybe I'll be able to do something for you someday."

That made the lion laugh. "You? Do something for me? That's a joke!" But he was amused by the little mouse, so he let him go.

The next day, the lion got caught in a trap. The hunters tied the lion to a tree while they went to get a cart to carry him away. The lion roared and the little mouse heard him. He laughed with delight. "Now the lion knows how it feels to be captured and helpless," the little mouse thought, and he smiled.

Alternative Endings

Read the folk tale with its familiar ending. Then use complete sentences to write an alternative ending.

The Little Red Hen

The little red hen found a grain of wheat and asked, "Who will plant this wheat?"

"Not I," said the goose.

"Not I," said the duck.

"Then I will," said the little red hen.

When the wheat was ripe, the little red hen asked, "Who will take this wheat to the mill?"

"Not I," said both the goose and the duck.

"Then I will," said the little red hen.

When the wheat was ground into flour, the little red hen asked, "Who will make some bread with this flour?"

"Not I," said the goose and the duck.

"Then I will," said the little red hen.

And when the bread was baked to a golden brown, the little red hen asked, "Who will eat this bread?"

"I will!" said the goose.

"I will!" said the duck.

But the little red hen smiled and said, "No, I shall eat it myself." And she did.

Alternative ending: _____

_____

_____

_____

_____

_____

_____

Problem and Solution

Most stories have a problem, something that needs to be fixed.

> Mark needed the dictionary, but it was on the top shelf and he couldn't reach it.

The solution is the way to fix it.

> Mark used a stool to stand on to reach the dictionary.

> Read the stories and identify the problem and solution.

I Can't Be Late
Rosie needed to catch the bus to town at 8:30. She was afraid she would oversleep and miss the bus. So she set her alarm clock to be sure she would get up in time.

Problem: _____

_____

Solution: _____

_____

Hurry Before It Melts!
Jason got a popsicle out of the freezer. After he unwrapped it and started to eat it, his mother asked him to go get the mail. Jason put the popsicle back in the freezer and headed to the mailbox.

Problem: _____

_____

Solution: _____

_____

Problem and Solution

Read the story and identify the problem and solution.

Just Enough Mittens

Mercedes and Elena wanted to build a snowman. Mercedes could only find one mitten. Elena looked in her closet and found three mittens. She gave one mitten to Mercedes, so they both had two mittens.

Problem: _____

_____

Solution: _____

_____

Now write your own story and identify the problem and solution.

Title: _____

_____

_____

_____

_____

_____

Problem: _____

_____

Solution: _____

_____

Compare and Contrast

Use the choice box to describe
how each set of things are alike.

furniture	subjects	people
plants	drive-in food	countries
trees	places to eat	boxers
body parts	~~jewelry~~	dogs

1. earrings   necklace   ring   _j e w e l r y_

2. maple   pine   oak   _____

3. arms   legs   hands   _____

4. sofa   table   chair   _____

5. science   reading   math   _____

6. restaurant   kitchen   diner   _____

7. beagle   poodle   collie   _____

8. Russia   Canada   Mexico   _____

Compare and Contrast

Use the choice box to describe
how each set of things are alike.

clothing	face parts	measurements
coats	months	shapes
parts of a paragraph	March	rectangle
parts of a sentence	relatives	tools

1. punctuation   sentence   word   _____

2. jacket   shirt   sweater   _____

3. drill   hammer   screwdriver   _____

4. aunt   brother   father   _____

5. foot   inch   yard   _____

6. circle   square   triangle   _____

7. jaw   lip   teeth   _____

8. April   May   August   _____

Compare and Contrast

In each row below the choice box, cross out the word that does not belong. Then use the choice box to describe how the two items are alike.

bodies of water	on your head	toe
chair	parts of the year	valley
ways to cook	relatives	~~wear on feet~~
liquids	times of the day	window covers

1. boots   ~~gloves~~   shoes   <u>wear on feet</u>

2. boil   fry   freeze   _____

3. sandwich   juice   water   _____

4. ocean   river   mountain   _____

5. ear   eye   finger   _____

6. curtains   drapes   sofa   _____

7. aunt   cousin   friend   _____

8. month   morning   afternoon   _____

Compare and Contrast

In each row below the choice box, cross out the word that does not belong. Then use the choice box to describe how the two items are alike.

banana	fruit	things that fasten
bodies of water	may	units of time
days of week	minute	tools
have four legs	months	winter

1. deer   duck   rabbit   _____

2. button   zipper   mouth   _____

3. fall   July   June   _____

4. cloud   lake   river   _____

5. day   hour   third   _____

6. Friday   January   Tuesday   _____

7. hammer   saw   comb   _____

8. lemon   orange   squash   _____

Ordering

Number the objects from smallest to largest. Then number the same group from largest to smallest.

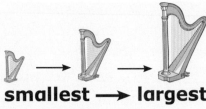

smallest ➞ largest

largest ➞ smallest

_____ moose	_____ moose
_____ frog	_____ frog
_____ elephant	_____ elephant
___1___ ant	_____ ant
_____ raccoon	___4___ raccoon
_____ tiger	_____ tiger

Ordering

Number the objects from smallest to largest. Then number the same group from largest to smallest.

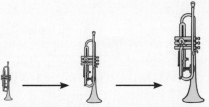

smallest → largest

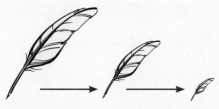

largest → smallest

_____ sea	_____ sea
_____ pond	_____ pond
_____ ocean	_____ ocean
_____ drop	_____ drop
_____ lake	_____ lake
_____ puddle	_____ puddle

Ordering

Number the objects from largest to smallest. Then number the same group from smallest to largest.

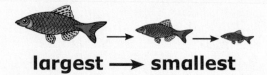

largest → smallest

smallest → largest

_____ basketball	_____ basketball
_____ pea	_____ pea
_____ ping-pong ball	_____ ping-pong ball
_____ plum	_____ plum
_____ baseball	_____ baseball
_____ marble	_____ marble

Ordering

Number the objects from largest to smallest. Then number the same group from smallest to largest.

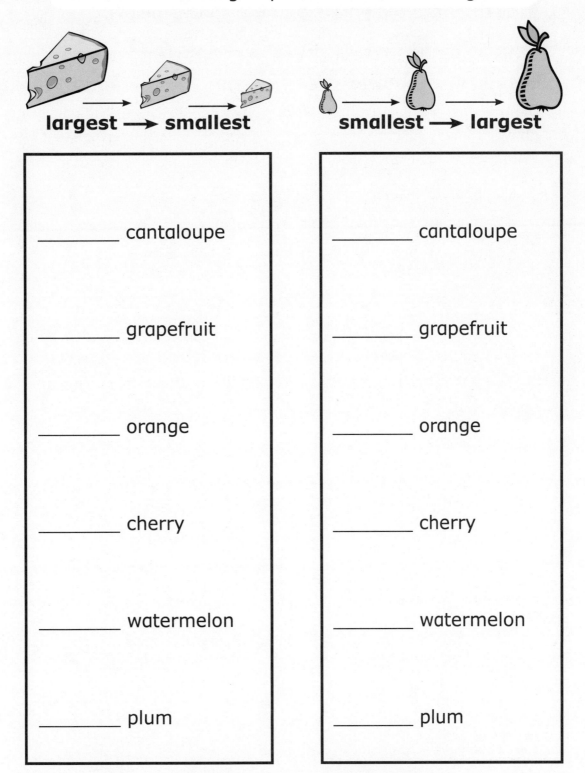

largest ⟶ smallest   smallest ⟶ largest

_____ cantaloupe	_____ cantaloupe
_____ grapefruit	_____ grapefruit
_____ orange	_____ orange
_____ cherry	_____ cherry
_____ watermelon	_____ watermelon
_____ plum	_____ plum

Categorizing

Sort the list of words according to animals that fly, animals that swim, and animals that do both. Write the answers in the spaces below.

bass	eagle	wren	swan
bat	gull	raven	walrus
crow	goose	seal	whale
duck	salmon	shark	robin

Swim

Swim and Fly

Fly

Categorizing

Sort the list of words according to the number of legs the animal has. Write the answers in the spaces below.

Animals

cat	snake
bird	goose
squirrel	fish
dog	worm
chicken	bear

Categories

Has two legs	Has four legs	Has zero legs
_____	_____	_____
_____	_____	_____
_____	_____	_____
	_____	

Sequencing

A **sequence** is the order in which things happen, are carried out, or are arranged.

Monday, Tuesday, Wednesday, Thursday, Friday, Saturday, Sunday

Use the choice box to answer each question.

1. What day is it today, if yesterday was Monday?

   _____

2. If today is Thursday, what day will it be tomorrow?

   _____

3. What day is it today, if yesterday was Saturday?

   _____

4. If today is Tuesday, what day will be tomorrow?

   _____

5. What day is it today, if tomorrow is Sunday?

   _____

6. If today is Monday, what day was yesterday?

   _____

7. What day is it today, if yesterday was Friday?

   _____

Sequencing

January, February, March, April, May, June, July, August, September, October, November, December

Use the choice box to answer each question.

1. What month is it, if last month was January?

   _____

2. If this month is February, what will next month be?

   _____

3. What month is it, if last month was June?

   _____

4. If this month is July, what will next month be?

   _____

5. What month is it, if last month was October?

   _____

6. If this month is November, what will next month be?

   _____

7. What month is it, if last month was April?

   _____

8. If this month is May, what will next month be?

   _____

Sequencing

Number the steps in the correct sequence.

_____ Soap the dog.

_____ Fill the tub with water.

___|___ Decide it's time to wash your dog.

_____ Dry the dog.

_____ Rinse the dog.

_____ Get the dog wet.

_____ Catch the dog for its bath.

Sequencing

Number the steps in the correct sequence.

_____ Take a shopping cart.

_____ Prepare a shopping list.

_____ Pay the cashier.

_____ Leave your house.

_____ Leave the store.

_____ Go to the store.

_____ Put all items in a shopping cart.

Sequencing

A **sequence** is the order in which things happen, are carried out, or are arranged.

> Sequence the events of the fairy tale, *Cinderella*, from first to last using the numbers 1 - 10.

_____ Cinderella lost her glass slipper when she was running from the castle.

_____ Cinderella was sad because she was not invited to the ball.

_____ Cinderella's fairy godmother appeared and gave her a beautiful dress.

_____ Cinderella's fairy godmother changed a pumpkin into a coach.

___1___ Cinderella's stepsisters were invited to the ball.

_____ The clock struck midnight.

_____ The prince and Cinderella danced at the ball.

___10___ The prince and Cinderella were married and lived happily ever after.

_____ The prince knew that he had found Cinderella because the glass slipper fit her foot.

_____ The prince found Cinderella's glass slipper and began searching for her.

Cause and Effect

When something happens, you can usually find a reason why it happened. The **cause** of an event is why something happened.

> Garrett had been looking forward to seeing the movie. He loaded the disc into his DVD player but then accidentally dropped the player. Since the player stopped working, Garrett did not get to watch the movie.

> In the above story, what caused Garrett not to be able to see the movie? Write a complete sentence.

_____

_____

It is important to make sure that one event really is the cause of another. While two events can happen at the same time, one event may not have directly caused the other.

> Garrett had been looking forward to seeing the movie. He loaded the disc into his DVD player but then accidentally dropped it. The player would no longer work. Just then his sister ran in the door, bumped into him, and knocked the player out of his hands and onto the floor.

> In the above story, what caused the player to stop working? Circle the best answer.

1. Garrett loading the disc.
2. Garrett's sister.
3. The first time the player was dropped on the floor.

Cause and Effect

When something happens, you can usually find a reason why it happened. The **cause** of an event is why something happened. Sometimes there can be a sequence of causes. One event causes the next event, which causes the next event, and so on.

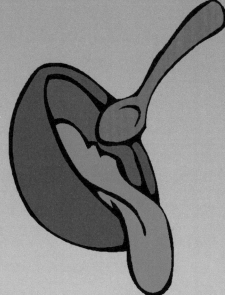

May opened a door that hit Mr. Cho. To catch his fall, Mr. Cho threw his hands out, causing him to drop the soup bowl.

What two events caused Mr. Cho to spill his soup?

1. _____

2. _____

Cause and Effect

Certain key words can help you recognize whether an event is a cause or an effect. These words are called signal words.

Signal words that can show cause are:

because	due to	since
caused by	led to	the reason
created by	on account of	

In each of the sentences below, circle the signal word(s) showing cause.

1. The reason Susan was late for class was that she missed the bus.

2. Susan was late for class on account of missing the bus.

3. Susan was late for class due to missing the bus.

4. Since it was getting dark, he went home.

5. A broken streetlight led to an auto accident.

6. Jim stayed home because he was afraid to ride in a plane.

7. The power outage was caused by the storm.

Cause and Effect

The **effect** is change that results from a cause. A cause can have more than one effect.

The Storm

Trees were blown down. Many buildings and cars were damaged. Whole houses were lifted in the air. All of this was caused by a tornado that hit our town.

List three effects caused by the storm.

1. _____

2. _____

3. _____

Cause and Effect

Certain key words can help you recognize whether an event is a cause or an effect. These words are called signal words.

Signal words that can show effect are:

as a result	so	since
finally	caused by	thus
because	then	therefore

In each of the sentences below, circle the signal word(s) showing effect.

1. The picnic was cancelled as a result of the rain.

2. They had to stop when their gas finally ran out.

3. Our car ran out of gas, thus we had to stop.

4. Mother wasn't home yet, so we couldn't go outside to play.

5. It was getting dark, therefore we went home.

6. We went inside, then it started to rain.

Prediction

A **prediction** is an inference that you make about what someone is going to do or something that is going to happen.

Uncle George

Uncle George was the kindest soul I ever knew. He was always helping people. If someone needed a hand, he could count on Uncle George. He had never said no to anyone. One day a stranger came to Uncle George's house after the stranger's car broke down.

Predict what will happen next in the story. Write complete sentences.

_____

_____

_____

_____

_____

_____

Prediction

Gloria and the Ride

Gloria climbed the steps slowly. She didn't want to try the ride. It was too high, it was too fast, and it was too scary. Just watching the cars was making her dizzy, so she made a decision.

Predict what Gloria will do. Write complete sentences.

_____

_____

_____

_____

_____

Context Clues

When you see a word you don't know, try using the other words around it to help you find the word's meaning. The other words that help give a word meaning are called **context clues**.

Read the following sentence and use the context clues in the sentence to help you find the meaning of <u>adorn</u>.

The girls will adorn their hair with flowers and ribbons.

Circle the meaning of <u>adorn</u>.

1. to make something beautiful
2. to attach something
3. wash

Sometimes a sentence will describe the meaning of a word.

Read the following sentence and use the context clues in the sentence to help you find the meaning of <u>perspiration</u>.

There was perspiration dripping from his hot face.

Circle the meaning of <u>perspiration</u>.

1. sweat
2. dryness
3. blood

Context Clues

When you see a word you don't know, try using the other words around it to help you find the word's meaning. The other words that help give a word meaning are called **context clues**. An exclamation mark can also be a clue.

Read the following sentence and use the context clues in the sentence to help you find the meaning of <u>railed</u>.

"You won't get away with this!" the angry man railed at the children.

Circle the meaning of <u>railed</u>.

1. said quietly
2. said with anger
3. said hopefully

Read the following paragraph and use the context clues in the paragraph to help you find the meaning of <u>cancelled</u>.

We were upset that the game was cancelled. It was the last game of the season. We wouldn't get another chance to play. I wish it hadn't rained!

Circle the meaning of <u>cancelled</u>.

1. played
2. called off
3. answer not given

Writing Detective ®

Handy Mandy

[1]Mandy had to hurry! [2]Her favorite TV show was about to start and it was Monday, which meant it was her turn to wash and dry the dishes. [3]If she had to do it all alone, she'd never get done in time to watch the show.

[4]Her sister, Katy, was sitting at the kitchen table doing her homework. [5]She was having a hard time answering one of the questions. [6]"Mandy, will you help me with this problem?" she asked her sister.

[7]That gave Mandy an idea. [8]"I will help you, Katy, if you will help me."

[9]"OK," Katy said, "what do I need to do?"

[10]"I'll work on the problem with you and then you can dry the dishes with me. [11]Does that sound fair?"

[12]Katy thought it was a good idea. [13]Soon, she had finished her homework, and not long after that, the dishes were done. [14]Mandy hurried into the living room. [15]She was just in time to watch her show!

Reading Questions

1. What sentence tells you where Katy was sitting? _____

2. What sentence tells you what Mandy's problem was ? _____

3. How do you think Mandy solved her problem?

    _____

    What sentence is the best evidence for your answer? _____

4. Number the events from 1–5 in the order they happened in the story.

    ____ Mandy was just in time to watch her TV show.

    ____ Katy was sitting at the kitchen table doing her homework.

    ____ It was Mandy's turn to wash and dry the dishes.

    ____ Mandy hurried into the living room.

    ____ Katy thought Mandy's idea was good.

Writing Detective®

Now that you've read the story and answered the questions, write a paragraph about what the story was about. Before you write your paragraph, look at the questions and make some notes about the story to guide you when you write.

1. Who is the story about? _____

2. What were they doing? _____

3. Where did this happen? _____

4. When did this happen? _____

5. How did Mandy solve her problem? _____

_____

_____

_____

_____

_____

_____

_____

_____

Writing and Following Directions

Always read and follow directions.

Find the first clue letter on the chart. Then move in the directions that the arrows point, one square for each arrow. After you complete each set of directions, write down the name of the letter you have stopped on.

A	H	W	D	O
G	T	Z	B	F
R	E	L	V	P
U	M	K	N	C

Example: L → ↑ ← = Z

Clues

1. G → → ↑ = _____

2. L → ↑ ↑ → = _____

3. Z ↓ ↓ → = _____

4. P ↑ ↑ ← = _____

5. W ← ↓ ↓ = _____

6. W ← ← ↓ ↓ = _____

7. L ↑ → → = _____

8. K ← ← = _____

9. U ↑ → → = _____

Write the word ___ ___ ___ ___ ___ ___ ___ ___ ___.

Writing and Following Directions

Always read and follow directions.

Find the mystery shape.

1. Inside the largest circle, write the numeral for the total number of shapes.

2. If your first answer is spelled with four letters, shade in the small triangle. If it's not, cross out the last two shapes.

3. The shape you are looking for has only straight lines.

4. Cross out the largest of each shape.

5. Cross out the shapes that have fewer than four sides.

6. Cross out the shapes that do not have four equal sides.

7. Put the numeral 1 above the mystery shape.

Draw the mystery shape.

Writing and Following Directions

Always read and follow the directions.

    a. Draw a circle above the arrow.
    b. Draw a square to the left of the arrow.
    c. Draw a triangle in the upper left corner.

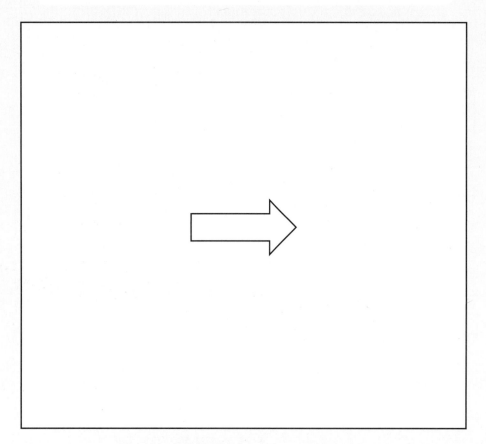

Circle the correct answers.

1. The triangle is **below - above** the square.

2. The circle is to the **right - left** of the triangle.

3. The **square - arrow - circle** is in the center.

Writing and Following Directions

Give the car directions to get to the house with two windows by circling the correct words that complete the sentences.

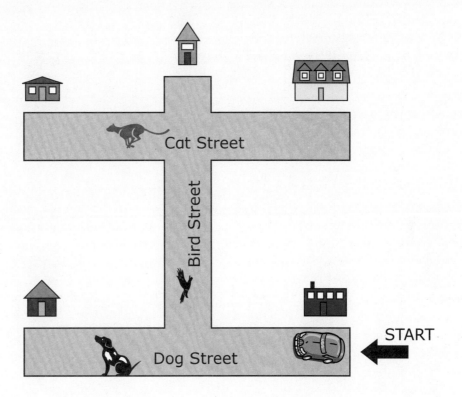

1. Drive on Dog Street to **Bat - Bird** Street.

2. Turn **left - right** on Bird Street.

3. Drive on Bird Street to **Cat - Cap** Street.

4. Turn **left - right** on **Bat - Cat** Street.

5. Drive on Cat Street to the end.

6. The house is on the **left - right** side of the street.

Writing and Following Directions

Give the car directions to get to the
house with the fewest windows.

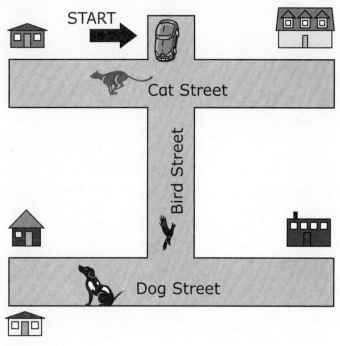

1. Drive on _____ Street to _____

    Street.

2. Turn _____ on _____
        (direction)

    _____.

3. Drive on _____ _____ to the end.

4. The house is on the _____ side of the
                              (right/left)

    _____.

Parts of a Book

Match each part of a book with its picture.

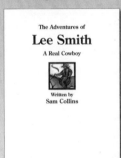

Front Cover

Protects the pages and identifies the title of the book.

Title Page

Identifies the title, author, publisher, and copyright.

Table of Contents

Identifies the chapters, sections, and sometimes topics in the book. It also tells you where to find these items in the book.

Glossary

A list of important words and terms found in the book. A glossary explains their meanings.

Point to each part of this *Language Smarts Level C* book.

   a. Front Cover

   b. Title Page

   c. Table of Contents

Parts of a Book

A **glossary** contains a list of important words and terms found in a book and explains their meanings.

Use the glossary to answer the questions about this book.

Glossary

 B

bedroll—A portable roll of bedding used especially by campers and others who sleep outdoors

 C

cattle drive—Moving a bovine herd (as cows or bulls or steers).

 J

jerkey—Dried meat used as trail rations.

 L

lasso—A long rope with a running noose at one end, used especially to catch horses and cattle.

 S

spurs—A short spike or spiked wheel that attaches to the heel of a rider's boot and is used to urge a horse forward.

The Adventures of

Lee Smith

A Real Cowboy

Written by
Sam Collins

1. Lee Smith probably carried a __ __ d __ __ __ __ in the story.

2. While on a cattle drive, Lee Smith probably used a __ __ __ __ __ to catch horses and cattle.

3. Lee Smith and the other cowboys probably ate __ __ __ __ __ __ while on the trail.

Parts of a Book

The **table of contents** identifies a book's chapters, sections, and sometimes topics. It also tells you where to find these items in the book.

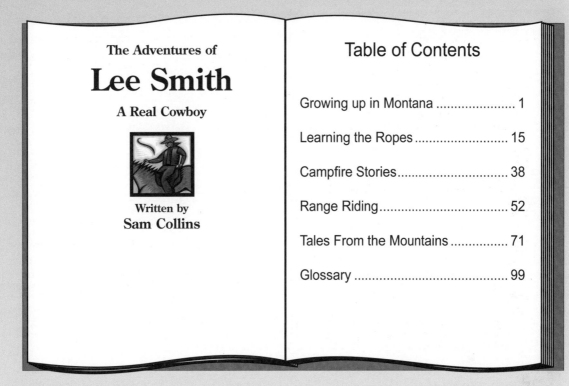

1. In which chapter would you read about the stories cowboys told while sitting around the campfire?

   _____

2. Which chapter tells you where Lee Smith lived when he was a boy? _____

3. If you are reading page 39, which chapter are you in?

   _____

Using the Dictionary

A dictionary explains the meanings of words.

H

hero
A person admired for great deeds or fine qualities. One who shows great courage.

heron
A wading bird that has long legs, a long neck, a long, thin bill; and large wings.

herring
A widely used food fish of the North Atlantic Ocean.

hers
That which belongs to her.

he's
Contraction; he is, he has

hexagon
A closed figure with six angles and six sides.

hey
Used to call attention or express excitement.

hi
Used as a greeting.

hibernate
To pass the winter in sleep. Bears hibernate.

hiccup
A gulping sound that follows a spasm of the diaphragm.

hickory
A tall tree related to the walnut that has strong wood and bears an edible nut.

Using the Dictionary

Use the dictionary page to answer the questions.

1. What is the word in the dictionary after the word "heron?"

_____

2. What are the words that have more than one meaning?

_____

3. Circle the word that would likely be found at the end

of the dictionary.   ant   bat   zoo

4. If the dictionary contained the word "bread," would it go

before or after the word "book?" _____

Choose a word from the dictionary page to complete the sentence.

5. That wading bird with the large wings is a

_____.

6. In math class, we drew a _____, a

six-sided figure.

7. Superman was a _____ who was admired for his

great deeds.

Friendly Letters

Friendly letters have 5 parts.

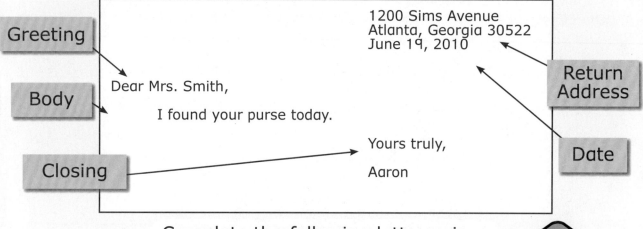

Greeting

Body

Closing

1200 Sims Avenue
Atlanta, Georgia 30522
June 19, 2010

Return Address

Date

Dear Mrs. Smith,

I found your purse today.

Yours truly,

Aaron

Complete the following letter using the items in the boxes below.

Dear Sarah,

34 Summer Lane
Boise, ID 83401

I am having a great time at summer camp.

Sincerely,

August 1, 2010

_____

_____

_____

_____

_____

_____

Mike

Friendly Letters

Use a comma after the greeting.

Use a comma between the city and state in your return address.

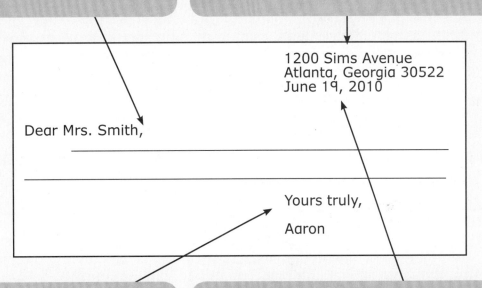

1200 Sims Avenue
Atlanta, Georgia 30522
June 19, 2010

Dear Mrs. Smith,

_____

_____

Yours truly,

Aaron

Use a comma after the closing.

Use a comma between the day of the month and the year.

Add 4 commas to complete the following letter.

637 White Avenue
Seattle Washington 98107
September 16 2010

Dear Sam

    I went to the park yesterday. I saw some white ducks
in the pond.

                         Yours truly

                         John

Friendly Letters

When someone gives you something special or does something nice for you, it is polite to write a thank-you note.

Use a comma

- between the city and state
- between the day of the month and the year
- after the greeting
- after the closing

Capitalize

- roads, cities, and states
- months, greetings
- names and titles of people
- first word in the closing

Circle 10 words that should be capitalized and add 4 commas.

3700 pacific avenue
boise idaho 89401
october 30 2010

dear mr. jones

   Thank you for reading my poem. I am glad you liked it.

                              sincerely

                              lisa

Friendly Letters

Circle 13 words that should be capitalized
and add 7 punctuation marks.

1700 pacific avenue
boise idaho 89401
may 7 2010

dear aunt susan

   thank you for the hat it will help me keep warm you are

sweet to remember my birthday

          yours truly

          lisa

Circle 12 words that should be capitalized.

4327 baker avenue
houston, texas 77025
february 13, 2010

dear aunt mary,

   thank you for letting me stay with you. it was fun to
play with your dogs.

         yours truly,

         eric

Friendly Letters

When someone gives you something special or does something nice for you, it is polite to write a thank-you note.

Circle 16 words that should be capitalized and add 8 punctuation marks.

1200 brown avenue
new york city new york
may 7 2010

dear mr smith

    thank you for the book i like to read you are kind to

remember my birthday

        yours truly

        aaron

Write a thank-you note to thank someone for a gift.

_____

_____

_____

_____

_____

_____

_____

_____

Friendly Letters

Formal English is used in serious letters.

> I will be delighted to meet you, Mr. Jones, when your plane arrives.

Informal English is used in personal letters.

> It's going to be great to see you! I can't wait until you get here!

Read each sentence and circle if it is formal or informal English.

1. Please respond immediately.   Formal   Informal

2. Give me a call when you get home.   Formal   Informal

3. I must insist on your cooperation.   Formal   Informal

4. Well, are we heading to the beach?   Formal   Informal

5. This rain is driving me crazy!   Formal   Informal

6. That pie was mmm-mmm good!   Formal   Informal

7. I congratulate you on your achievement. Formal   Informal

8. Way to go!   Formal   Informal

9. I have decided to make this purchase.   Formal   Informal

10. Yep, I'm going to buy it.   Formal   Informal

Friendly Letters

Formal English is used in serious letters.
Informal English is used in personal letters.

Write a letter to someone in your home about
a topic of your choice. Use informal English.

Write a letter to your teacher or principal about
your favorite subject. Use formal English.

Friendly Letters

An **e-mail** is a letter sent from a computer over the Internet. There are seven parts to a friendly e-mail.

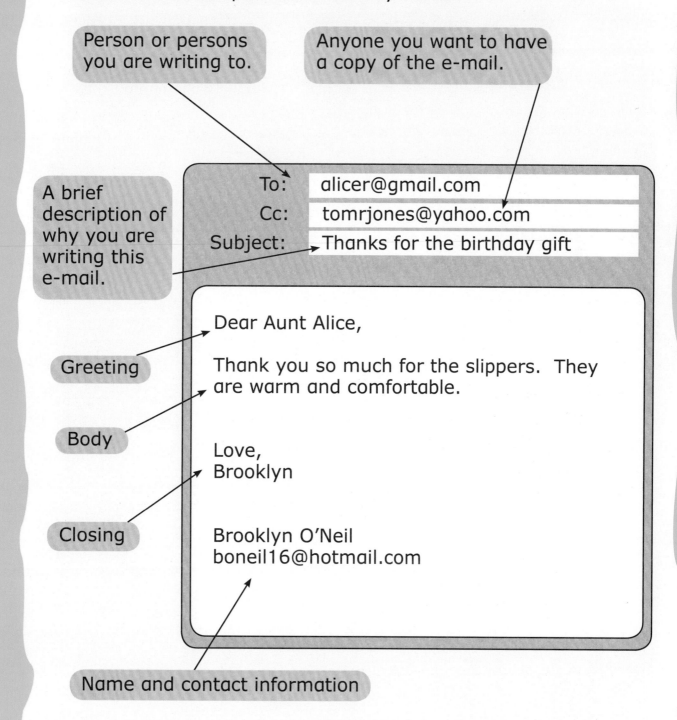

Person or persons you are writing to.

Anyone you want to have a copy of the e-mail.

A brief description of why you are writing this e-mail.

To: alicer@gmail.com

Cc: tomrjones@yahoo.com

Subject: Thanks for the birthday gift

Dear Aunt Alice,

Thank you so much for the slippers. They are warm and comfortable.

Love,
Brooklyn

Brooklyn O'Neil
boneil16@hotmail.com

Greeting

Body

Closing

Name and contact information

Friendly Letters

An **e-mail** is a letter sent from a computer over the Internet. There are seven parts to a friendly e-mail.

Write an e-mail to thank Donna for a gift she sent you.

To: donnak25@yahoo.com

Cc:

Subject:

_____

_____

_____

_____

_____

_____

_____

_____

Friendly Letters

Envelopes have three parts. The envelope below is a letter from Judy.

Draw a line to connect each part with its example below.

address, return address, stamp

Judy Smith
64 Thomas Avenue
Atlanta, Georgia 30522

Jerald Black
46 Smith Street
Atlanta, Georgia 30522

Friendly Letters

Envelopes have three parts.

address, return address, stamp

Fill in the 2 missing commas and circle the 12 words that should be capitalized on each envelope.

judy smith
64 thomas avenue
atlanta georgia 30522

jerald black
46 smith street
atlanta georgia 30522

ann perry
32 post street
seattle washington 98107

robert white
6749 ocean avenue
hanford california 93230

Friendly Letters

Use a comma

- between the city and state
- between the day of the month and the year
- after the greeting
- after the closing

Capitalize

- roads, cities, and states
- months and greetings
- names and titles of people
- first word in the closing

Fill in the 2 missing commas and circle the 12 words that should be capitalized on each envelope.

maya jones
45 beacon avenue
dallas texas 40404

simon george
63 oak street
atlanta georgia 30522

jennifer toledo
8 pleasant way
hanford california 93230

angela moyer
25 concord circle
armona california 93202

Friendly Letters

Address the envelope to yourself. Then circle 6 words that should be capitalized and add 1 comma in the return address.

judy smith
64 thomas avenue
atlanta georgia 30522

1

_____

_____

_____

Address this envelope to someone you know and use your address as the return address.

1

_____

_____

_____

_____

_____

_____

Writing

There are four steps in writing:

1. Gather and organize information and ideas.
2. Compose a written draft.
3. Edit your writing.
4. Revise your writing.

Fill in the blanks to complete each step.

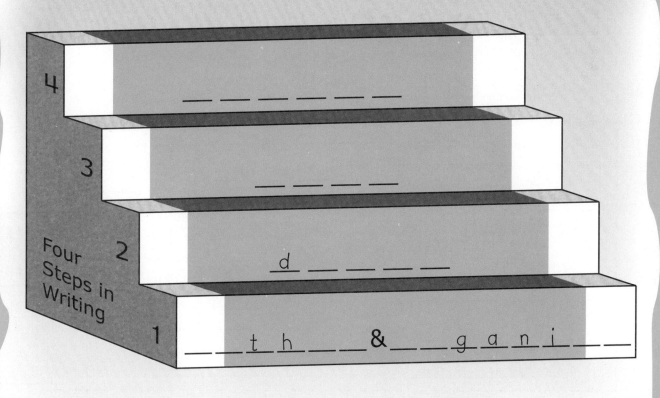

Four Steps in Writing

4 _ _ _ _ _ _ _

3 _ _ _ _

2 d _ _ _ _ _

1 _ _ t _ h _ _ & _ _ g a n i _ _ _

Writing

There are four steps in writing:
1. Gather and organize information and ideas.
2. Compose a written draft.
3. Edit your writing.
4. Revise your writing.

The first step is to gather and organize information and ideas.
- Brainstorm possible topics.
- Decide on who or what you want to write about.
- Organize ideas and collect information.

Four Steps in Writing
4 Revise
3 Edit
2 Draft
1 Gather & Organize

Write two things you could teach a pet.

_____

_____

List the steps you would take for each.

_____   _____

_____   _____

_____   _____

_____   _____

Writing

The second step is to compose a written draft.
- The beginning introduces the subject.
- The middle should explain and support your idea.
- The end should remind the reader why the subject is important.

> Write a warning to your friends that there is something dangerous in your backyard.

Title: _____

Beginning: _____

_____

_____

Middle: _____

_____

_____

End: _____

_____

_____

Writing

There are four steps in writing:
1. Gather and organize information and ideas.
2. Compose a written draft.
3. Edit your writing.
4. Revise your writing.

The third step is to edit.
- Is my idea easy to understand?
- Do I need to add anything?
- Do I need to take any parts out?
- Do I have my sentences in the right order?

Identify the 4 steps when planning a party and number them 1-4.

_____ Set a date and time for the party.

_____ Get permission to have a party.

_____ Send out invitations.

_____ Decorate for the party.

Writing

The fourth step is to revise. Ask yourself the following questions:

- Have I used the correct punctuation?
- Have I spelled everything correctly?
- Did I use correct grammar?

Circle the 3 punctuation errors, 2 capitalization errors, and 2 grammatical errors in the letter.

24 Olympic St
Seattle, Washington 98107
May 3, 2010

Dear Mary

    I am hardly not having a good time at my aunt's house. It has rained everyday monday was the worst day. I will see you soon!

        yours truly,

        Jennifer

Writing

Use the following four steps to write a short story about the picture (below).

1. Gather and organize information and ideas about your story.

   _____

   _____

   _____

   _____

2. Compose a written draft.

   _____

   _____

   _____

3. Edit your draft.

4. Revise your writing.

   _____

   _____

   _____

Writing

Use the following four steps to write a short story about the picture (below).

1. Gather and organize information and ideas.

   _____

   _____

   _____

   _____

2. Compose a written draft.

   _____

   _____

   _____

3. Edit your draft.

4. Revise your writing.

   _____

   _____

   _____

   _____

Writing

Use the following four steps to write a
short story about the picture (below).

1. Gather and organize information and
    ideas.

    _____

    _____

    _____

    _____

2. Compose a written draft.

    _____

    _____

    _____

3. Edit your draft.

4. Revise your writing.

    _____

    _____

    _____

Writing

Use the following four steps to write a short story about the picture (below).

1. Gather and organize information and ideas.

_____

_____

_____

_____

2. Compose a written draft.

_____

_____

_____

3. Edit your draft.

4. Revise your writing.

_____

_____

_____

Answers

Page 1

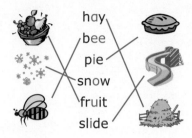

hay
bee
pie
snow
fruit
slide

Page 2 cake
ocean
key
kite
uniform

Page 3

	Examples
unicorn	mule
key	bee
cone	bone
plane	paint
lion	pile

Page 4

2. The ducks were swimming in the lake. long a
3. Three children went to the school party. long e
4. Mary closed her book and left the room. long o
5. That puppy is awfully cute. long u
6. Mark painted the walls in his room red. long a
7. Mike finished his lunch quickly. long i
8. An elephant led the circus parade. long a
9. The farmer will grow apples and carrots. long o

Page 5

long a	long e	long i
name	free	wide
may	we	time
make	see	mine
way	bean	hive

long o	long u
grow	tube
snow	cute
boat	use
load	music

Page 6

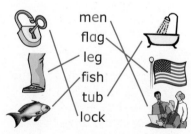

men
flag
leg
fish
tub
lock

Page 7 pig
nest
duck
cat
dog

Page 8

	Examples
fox	box
drum	sum
cap	dad
bed	jet
chicken	fit

Page 9

2. I see a big gray whale, Kate! short i
3. I may race, not skate. short o
4. Jane baked a nice apple pie. short a
5. I see a snake on a crate. short o
6. May I name a crane Bob? short o
7. I hiked like Mike, but I became lame. short u
8. I spied nine vines winding down a pine. short o
9. Fred waves while he shaves. short e

Page 10

short a	short e	short i
glad	melt	twig
pack	jet	fin
that	shed	will
bag	send	flip

short o	short u
block	shut
mock	mug
trot	mutt
pots	mud

Page 11

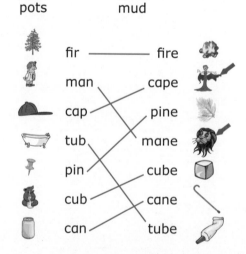

fir —— fire
man   cape
cap   pine
tub   mane
pin   cube
cub   cane
can   tube

Page 12

2. The car has a flat tire.
3. Sara is eight and her friend, Tim, is nine.
4. I located North America on the globe.

5. She handed me a grape popsicle.
6. He played a tune on the piano.
7. I talked to my brother on the phone.
8. My dad gave me a puppy on my birthday.

Page 13
2. I got mad when my mom made me do my homework.
3. I bit the candy bar and then gave my brother a bite.
4. Jane and Emily slid down the slide.
5. My mother sent a note saying I was not to go outside.
6. The guy who tried to rob the bank was wearing a robe.
7. Jason cut in line to stand next to the cute girl.
8. The teacher told us to use pens and not pencils on the test.
9. Ben's grandmother gave him a huge hug!

Page 14
2. I will race you to the gate at the lake!
3. Take your bike and ride to the cave.
4. I hope he brings a rope.
5. I ate cake for lunch.
6. My kite got tangled in the tall pine.
7. Two mice were in the bag of rice.
8. The nose on his face was huge and red.
9. I will use my cape to put out this fire!
10. It was nice to skate on the ice.

Page 15
star
tornado
nurse
weather
girl

Page 16
	Examples
farm	barn
feather	sister
bird	first
door	fork
turkey	hurt

Page 17
surf	tiger
arm	jar
fork	shark
horse	skirt
butter	
hamburger	

Page 18
2. When it got dark, he turned on the lights.
3. My brother is the best soccer

player on the team.
4. The dog had a thorn in its foot and it hurt.
5. John put the paper in the third drawer.
6. My sister plays the harp.
7. I like lots of butter on my corn.
8. He drove the large cart through the dirt.
9. I took a jar of water with me to the park.

Page 19
		Examples
ar	~~pie~~	barn
or	~~claw~~	born
er	~~dime~~	after
ir	~~toys~~	sir
ur	~~pillow~~	burn
ar	~~grape~~	far
er	~~tape~~	germ
or	~~boy~~	story
ir	~~blouse~~	girl

Page 20
goat
beach
hay
tree
mail
pie

Page 21
	Examples
sheep	deep
beaver	east
soap	boat
play	clay
snail	hail
fries	skies

Page 22
		Examples
2. tries	i	pies
3. boat	o	goat
4. green	e	bee
5. grain	a	chain
6. boast	o	toast
7. beach	e	bean
8. fail	a	pail

Page 23
2. May wore ribbons on her braids.
3. His knee hurt and walking was painful.
4. Jeff grabbed the soap and tried to wash the dog.
5. I am taking a trip to the East Coast today.
6. The old dog always stayed by the little goat.
7. I need to lie on the beach and soak up some sun.
8. The seal swam up to the boat the next day.
9. I used my green crayon and red paint.

Page 24   paint
sheep
peach
crayon
coat
wheel

Page 25   newspaper
paw
boy
crown
cloud
soil
spoon
auto

Page 26

	Examples
clown	brown
boy	toy
mouse	loud
goose	loose
oil	boil
saw	straw
auto	laundry
foot	good

Page 27   2. This soil is good for growing roses.
3. Grab a broom and help me.
4. Sarah had a frown on her face.
5. The lamp will work after I screw in this lightbulb.
6. I checked a book out of the library.
7. That cat has sharp claws!
8. Sadie sat down to play with her toys.
9. It got cold, so Julie went into the house.

Page 28   screw   **Page 29**   moose
fawn   paw
coins   couch
balloon   crown
cookie   crawl
yawn   stool

Page 30

	Examples
fish	Friday, fry, farm
ball	barn, balloon, bake
dolphin	dog, dad, dish

Page 31

	Examples
hammer	her, has, hay
jam	jump, jar, jelly
kite	kitten, kick, kind
light	lick, like, life

Page 32

	Examples
man	mad, mom, magic
rope	ran, ring, red
pig	park, peel, pear

Page 33   pretzel
plane
swim
grapes
smile
snow

Page 34   block
flower
frog
crab
dress
brain

Page 35   stairs
spear
glove
square
snail
skunk
tree

Page 36   plane
glove
grapes
sleep
school

Page 37   stop
skunk
snake
spoon
smile
snow
swim

Page 38

	Examples
ch	chin
ck	lock
ph	photo
sh	shop
th	three
wh	where

Page 39   cheese
inch
trophy
shadow
lock
whistle

Page 40

	Examples
dolphin	phony
chair	charm
whale	white
thumb	that
truck	rock
sheep	ship

Page 41
One elephant
One sheep
One chicken
One whale
One sloth
Cook for three days.
Quickly add three
blocks of cheese.

Page 42
1. Phone your friends.
2. Ask them to join you at three o'clock after the quiz.
3. When your friends arrive, give them a big bowl of soup topped with cheese.
4. When you are finished, put the leftover soup in a big refrigerator.

Page 43
by
dry
fly
July
spy
sty
fry

Page 44
physical
myth
syllable
Egypt
rhythm

Page 45
yahoo
yummy
yawn
yolk
yarn
young

Page 46
1. pig
2. cat
3. ze • bra
4. chick • en
5. but • ter • fly
6. al • li • ga • tor

Page 47
1. harp
2. horn
3. drum
4. gui • tar
5. pi • an • o
6. xy • lo • phone
7. ban • jo

Page 48
com • put • er
can • dle
rac • coon
sand • wich
um • brel • la
ba • nan • a

Page 49
1. Teresa
2. Mark

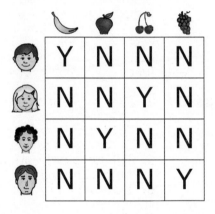

	Mark	Debbie	Teresa	Bradley
	N	Y	N	N
	Y	N	N	N
	N	N	Y	N
	N	N	N	Y

Page 50
1. banana   grapes
2. apple   cherries

	Y	N	N	N
	N	N	Y	N
	N	Y	N	N
	N	N	N	Y

Page 51

at family	an family
cat	tan
mat	pan
rat	can
hat	fan
sat	ran

et family	en family
met	ten
pet	pen
jet	den
net	hen
wet	men

in family	ip family
fin	hip
thin	lip
chin	trip
pin	drip
win	slip

Page 52

og family	ub family
dog	cub
jog	hub
hog	sub
frog	rub
log	tub

ock family
mock
sock
dock
rock
clock

ug family
bug
mug
chug
lug
rug

ock family
clock
knock
block
mock
shock

ump family
lump
dump
plump
grump
bump

ate family
late
hate
state
mate
fate

and family
band
sand
and
hand
land

Page 56 Examples

pale	gale	sale
late	gate	date
deep	sleep	weep
nest	rest	best
hide	side	ride
will	fill	hill
line	mine	fine
white	write	bite
block	clock	shock

Page 53 Examples

ran	can	fan
pet	jet	net
pen	ten	men
pin	fin	win
lip	drip	slip
jog	dog	log
sock	rock	clock
tub	cub	sub
mug	rug	bug

Page 57
blue
brown
green
red
white
yellow

Page 54

ale family
sale
pale
male
whale
gale

ate family
gate
late
date
mate
rate

Page 58
two
three
four
five

four
three
two
one

est family
best
jest
nest
pest
rest

ite family
bite
write
white
polite
site

Page 59

after
girl
first
go
in
little
new
off
work

big
last
before
old
on
out
play
stop
boy

ine family
fine
dine
line
pine
mine

ide family
ride
bride
hide
side
tide

girl	boy
little	big
go	stop

Page 55

ake family
bake
cake
lake
take
wake

ill family
thrill
pill
will
fill
hill

Page 60

1. around
2. because
3. don't
4. funny
5. sleep
6. went

1. always
2. buy
3. for
4. look
5. right
6. were

eep family
sleep
sheep
weep
beep
deep

eet family
sheet
sweet
feet
beet
fleet

1. and
2. round
3. soon
4. think
5. very
6. which

Page 61
1. any
2. going
3. me
4. our
5. please
6. those

1. an
2. into
3. open
4. pretty
5. up
6. we

1. as
2. could
3. is
4. know
5. not
6. over

Page 62
2. You will
3. She will
4. He will
5. They will
6. We will

Page 63
2. can't
3. don't
4. wouldn't
5. aren't
6. isn't
Sentences will vary.

Page 64
2. They've
3. We've
4. You've
5. They've
6. We've
Sentences will vary.

Page 65
1. You're
2. They're
3. We're
4. He's
5. She's
6. It's
Sentences will vary.

Page 66
not	have
not	are
not	have
is	are
will	is
am	not
is	will
is	have

Page 67
are + not	they + are
can + not	they + have
do + not	we + are
he + is	we + have
I + will	who + is
I + am	would + not
it + is	you + will
she + is	you + have

Page 68
1. base + ball = baseball
2. bed + room = bedroom
3. bee + hive = beehive
4. black + bird = blackbird
5. book + mark = bookmark
6. cow + boy = cowboy

Page 69
1. doorbell
2. eyeglasses
3. firefly
4. flowerpot
5. football
6. goldfish

Page 70
1. notebook
2. rainbow
3. pigtail
4. raincoat
5. boxcar
6. doghouse

Page 71
7. handbag
8. thumbnail
9. pancake
10. handshake
11. sandbox
12. lighthouse
13. sunflower
14. starfish

Page 72
1. eye + glasses
2. bull's + eye
3. cheer + leader
4. foot + ball
5. lady + bug
6. mail + box

Page 73
7. butter + fly
8. basket + ball
9. wheel + barrow
10. rain + bow
11. bath + tub
12. skate + board

Page 74
2. weep
3. pal
4. happy
5. mitt
6. nice
7. big
8. giggle
9. raise
10. angry
11. gift

Page 75
2. wealthy
3. bag
4. frighten
5. close
6. ill
7. easy
8. nap
9. creep
10. noise
11. rock

Page 76
1. hit
   smacked
   smashed
2. grumpy
   mad
   furious
3. clever
   smart
   brilliant
4. microscopic
   tiny
   small
5. said
   yelled
   roared
6. OK
   good
   perfect

Page 77
7. damp
   wet
   soggy
8. messy
   dirty
   filthy
9. bad
   awful
   terrible
10. ask
    request
    beg
11. fast
    quick
    speedy
12. slim
    thin
    scrawny
13. unkind
    mean
    evil

Page 78
2. back
3. little
4. top
5. open
6. night
7. full
8. sad
9. soft
10. cold
11. new

Page 79
2. up
3. wet
4. smile
5. empty
6. out
7. small
8. day
9. closed
10. happy
11. well
12. float

Page 80
1. 3
2. 6
3. 6, 9, 10
4. 4, 1, 2, 3

Page 81   Sentences will vary.

Page 82   misconduct/wrong behavior
disagree/do not agree
extraordinary/fantastic or amazing
nonsense/does not make sense
overwork/to work too much

Page 83
2. overcook
3. distrust
4. misunderstand
5. nonviolent
Sentences will vary.

Page 84   helper/one who helps
wonderful/full of wonder
hopeless/without hope
breakable/able to be broken
enjoyment/the act of enjoying

Page 85
2. dependable
3. helpless
4. grateful
5. commitment
Sentences will vary.

Page 86   teacher
dependable
excitement
helpless
hopeful

Page 87   disagree
overwork
mistrust
extraterrestrial

Page 88
December	February	Thursday
Father's Day	Wednesday	Monday
Christmas	Halloween	November
Memorial Day	January	April
New Year's Day	March	Friday
Independence Day	Sunday	Tuesday
Columbus Day	Saturday	August
Mother's Day	October	July
Presidents' Day	September	Easter
June	Thanksgiving	

Holidays
Father's Day
Christmas
Halloween
Memorial Day
New Year's Day
Independence Day
Easter
Columbus Day
Mother's Day
Presidents' Day
Thanksgiving

Months
December
February
November
January
April
March
August
October
July
September
June
July

Days of the Week
Thursday
Wednesday
Monday
Friday
Tuesday
Saturday
Sunday

Page 89
Solomon Grundy,
Born on Monday,
Christened on Tuesday,
Married on Wednesday,
Took ill on Thursday,
Worse on Friday,
Died on Saturday,
Buried on Sunday.
This is the end
Of Solomon Grundy.

Wednesday
Tuesday
Monday
Saturday
Sunday
Friday

Page 90
Thirty days hath September,
April, June, and November;
February has twenty-eight alone,
All the rest have thirty-one,
Excepting leap year, that's the time
When February's days are twenty-nine.

12
January, March, May, July, August,
October, December

April, June, September, November
February

Page 91
1. Tuesday is my birthday and I am excited.
2. My name is Robert and my nickname is Bob.
3. My dad's name is Sam. G. Brown.
4. I go to Dr. Larry Smith.
5. I am a Boy Scout.
6. "Little Red Riding Hood" is my favorite tale.
7. The United States is my home.

Page 92
My name is Thomas, and my nickname is Buddy. My next birthday will be on Christmas Day, Tuesday, December 25. I live in the United States. My dad is Sam G. Smith. He works with the Boy Scouts. My mother is Dr. Janet Smith. She works at the hospital.

Page 93   Stories will vary.

Page 94
Mary is my sister. She goes to Kennedy Elementary School and her teacher's name is Susan A. Jones. Tomorrow is Memorial Day and Mary and I are going on a picnic with my friend, Rocky. On Tuesday, we will read "Cinderella."

New Year's Day is January 1. My family always goes skiing on Mount Baler. My ski instructor's name is Tony S. Brown. I like him. He brings his dog, Fido, with him. He and I play in the snow.

Page 95   Sentences will vary.

Page 96
1. Sharks are good swimmers in the ocean.
2. I like to go to the ocean to swim.
3. I like to play in the ocean.

Page 97
1. Jim is a good student. He got all B's.
2. Tom is an average runner. Tom is faster than Lee.
3. Pam is taller than Maria. Pam is shorter than Nel.

Page 98   Sentences and fragments will vary.

Page 99
1. Grant is a picky eater. He does not like carrots.
2. Grant is a picky eater. He does not like peas.
3. Grant is a good reader. He likes stories about sports.

Page 100 1. I like to go to the park. We play ball.
2. I like to go to the pool. We swim all day.
3. I like to go to the store. We always buy gum.

Page 101 1. Grant is a good eater. He likes corn.
2. Grant is a good swimmer. He likes racing.
3. Grant is good at math. He likes to subtract.

Page 102 2. run-on
Grant is a good hiker. He likes to hike.
3. run-on
I like to go to the park. We play ball.
4. fragment
I like to play in the park.
5. fragment
I like to swim in the ocean.

Page 103 Sentences will vary.

Page 104 Sentences will vary.

Page 105 1. A funny person made us laugh.
2. Jim and I like to play.
3. A mean dog tried to bite me.
4. Jim and I like to climb trees.
5. Jim tells lots of jokes.
6. My brother and I have two little puppies.

Page 106 Paragraph will vary.

Page 107 Paragraph will vary.

Page 108 Paragraph will vary.

Page 109 Paragraph will vary.

Page 110 Paragraph will vary.

Page 111 2 Topic sentence
5 Supporting sentence
1 Supporting sentence
3 Supporting sentence
4 Closing sentence

My Best Birthday Party
The best birthday party I ever had was when I turned six. My mom and dad took my friends and me to the swimming pool. We swam and took turns jumping in and splashing! Then we had cake and I got some great presents. It was the best birthday party ever!

Page 112 Examples
cat, shirt, pants, shoes
shoes, pants, child or person
spaceship, flag, moon
teacher, girls, glasses

Page 113 Sentences will vary.

Page 114 2. Maryanne kicked the ball to Lynn.
3. Jeremy went to see Dr. Scott.
4. Tina loves to feed the birds.
5. Bobby ate all of Fred's dessert.
6. The band played at Mary's party.

Page 115 2. Susan has three dogs.
3. Kendell lives in that house.
4. My cat caught a mouse.
5. The chicken crossed the road.
6. Larry ate a peach and a pear.
7. Monica went to the Jackson Park.
8. Two men got off the bus.

Page 116
Person	Place
Billy	Peterson School
Jon	library
baby	outside
teacher	California
brother	park
doctor	office
Zoe	kitchen

Thing
skateboard
spoon
balloon
rock
tree
apple
book

Page 117 Sentences and nouns will vary.

Page 118 2. Bob, Bill, and Ted went to the park.
They went to the park.
3. The pillow is soft.
It is soft.
4. Jason went fishing.
He went fishing.
5. Molly loves chocolate.
She loves chocolate.
6. Anna and Grace play soccer.
They play soccer.

Page 119 2. It is a cute puppy.
3. She ate an apple.
4. They like to skate.
5. He will go to school tomorrow.
6. I can't wait for vacation.
7. We want to see that movie.
8. It is small and yellow.
9. Did they catch the bus?

Page 120 2. They like peanut butter and jelly sandwiches.
3. He is hungry.
4. She likes to eat peanut butter and jelly sandwiches.
5. He has a peanut butter and jelly sandwich every day.
6. Toby thinks making them is easy.
7. We all like to eat peanut butter and jelly sandwiches.

Page 121 The students listen.
The dog runs.

Page 122 Sentences and verbs will vary.

Page 123 Sentences and verbs will vary.

Page 124 2. The runners raced to the finish line.
3. The old dog snoozes in the sun.
4. The teacher read the book to the class.
5. The children laughed at the clowns.
6. Jennifer slipped on the icy sidewalk.
7. Jacob threw the ball to Sam.
Sentences will vary.

Page 125 2. At the picnic, most of the children swam in the lake.
3. Last night, I dreamed I was a race car driver.
4. The two girls climbed the tree and ate apples.
5. The students listened carefully to the teacher.
6. Lucy ran to her bedroom to get a sweater.
7. The swallows flew through the air.

Page 126 Sentences will vary.

Page 127 2. The boys rode their bikes to school. Past
3. My mother baked cookies for us. Past
4. I walk to my grandmother's house. Present
5. Morgan laughed at the clowns. Past
6. The puppy drinks the milk. Present
7. I buy lots of books. Present
8. The cat climbed the tree. Past

Page 128 1. I munch on potato chips. Present
2. Tim watched a movie. Past
3. I wash my face every morning. Present
4. The coach blew his whistle. Past
5. Sam climbed the tree. Past
6. Jason plays soccer. Present
7. The lion roared. Past
8. I walk to school. Present
9. The dog chews the bone. Present
10. Jim broke the window. Past
11. Leah sings very well. Present

Page 129 1. My cat jumps at the toy mouse I bought.
2. She will jump at it tomorrow, too.
3. She has jumped at it every time I have shown it to her.

1. My grandmother smiles whenever she sees me.
2. She smiled when I stopped by last week.
3. I know she will smile when she sees me tomorrow.

1. My cousin screams every time she sees a spider.
2. She screamed the last time she saw one.
3. I'm sure she will scream when she sees another one.

Page 130

```
 1       2
 a       d
 3
 d   a   r   e   d
 d       a
 e       4               8
 e       g   a   z   e   d       a
 d       g           9 p   e   t   t   e  10 d
         5 e   n   d   e  6 d       t       u
         d           7 r   a   c   e   d   s
                     i           n       t
                     e           d       e
                     d           e       d
                                 d
```

Across
3. I dared my brother to climb the tree.
4. I gazed up at the stars in the sky.
5. The teacher ended the lesson and left the room.
7. The girl raced to school because she was late.
9. James petted the little puppy.

Down
1. On the test, I added the rows of numbers.
2. Cody dragged the sled up the hill.
6. Nathan dried the dishes.
8. Emily attended the concert last night.
10. I dusted the books on my shelf.

Page 131   The bird flies.
The birds eat.

Page 132
2. He plays with trucks.
3. They play with trucks.
4. The girl plays with trucks.
5. She plays with a truck.
6. They play with trucks.
7. The girl and the boy play with trucks.

Page 133
1. The zebra is over there.
2. The pigs are over there.
3. The snake is over there.
4. The zebras are over there.
5. The pig is over there.
6. The snakes are over there.
7. The snake and the pigs are over there.
8. The zebras and the pigs are over there.

Page 134
1. 3
2. 12
3. He wasn't reading the directions correctly because he was distracted by the baseball game. 12
4. 3, 1, 4, 2, 5

Page 135   Paragraph will vary.

Page 136
2. The little bear ate the juicy berries.
3. The old man smiled at the cute little baby.
4. The two deer munched on the tender leaves.
5. I bought one ticket to the scary movie.
6. Nathan grabbed the big shovel, but I wanted one that was small.
7. The two girls watched as the three kittens played with the string.
8. He ate two sandwiches and a big red tomato.
9. Five cows munched on the green grass.

Page 137
2. My big toe hurts.
3. I ate the purple plum.
4. My mother made me some chocolate pudding.
5. Janell has three sisters.
6. The graceful swan glided across the lake.
New sentences will vary.

Page 138
1. His hair is shorter than mine is.
2. This race is more important.
3. Carl has the shortest hair.
4. Amy has the most beautiful hair.
5. I am a good reader, but Pat reads better. Carl is the best reader. Janet is a bad reader. Sam is worse than Janet. Tom is the worst reader.

Page 139
1. Today's test is more important than yesterday's.
2. Her pencil is shorter than mine.
3. Carl has the shortest pencil.
4. Amy has the most beautiful handwriting.
5. I am the best speller.
6. Of the three sisters, Penny is the oldest.
7. Jeremy is taller than I am.
8. I'm wearing the warmest coat I have.

9. This is the most delicious pizza I've ever eaten.
10. Today's game was more exciting than last week's game.

Page 140
1. Pat spells better than I.
2. Yesterday's test was more important than today's.
3. Yesterday's test was the most important test of the year.
4. Sam spelled more words correctly than Tom.
5. Sam is the best speller in the class.

Page 141 Mike is the best tennis player, but Beth is also good.
Kate is the worst tennis player because she is the only player Brad can beat.

Mike is taller than Beth, but both of them are shorter than Brad and Kate. Beth is the shortest.

Page 142 Today's game was shorter than yesterday's game. Sam hit a grand slam! He is the best player. We were not surprised that Tom did not even hit the ball. He is the worst baseball player, but he's really good at playing soccer. The most important game of the whole season is tomorrow. I will be the best player in that game!

Page 143
2. Patty happily hugged her grandfather.
3. The crowd cheered loudly.
4. The cows must be milked daily.
5. The fish swam slowly around the pool.
6. Nick pays his bills monthly.
7. The man yelled angrily at the boys.
8. Sarah will call tomorrow.
9. Jamie slurped his soda loudly.
10. The baby slept peacefully in his crib.

Page 144
2. We went to the park yesterday.
3. The woman yelled loudly at her children.
4. The cat ran quickly up the tree.
5. Alex does his homework nightly.
New sentences will vary.

Page 145
6. Sara walked carefully on the icy sidewalk.
7. The swan glided gracefully across the pond.

8. The three boys spoke quietly to each other.
9. My uncle visited us recently.
10. Suddenly, the car veered off the road.
11. The phone rang twice before I could answer it.
New sentences will vary.

Page 146
1. horses
2. bunnies
3. dishes
4. deer

Page 147 birds
bugs
dogs
pigs
cats

Page 148 cakes
doors
dresses
families
cows
wives
ladies
oxen
messes
mice
schools

Page 149 apples
babies
boxes
books
bunnies
cities
kisses
locks
lunches
shelves
parties
picnics
tomatoes
skies
stories

Page 150 pony
child
girl
sheep
goose
potato
deer
leaf
tooth
woman

Page 151 bus
chip
zebra
fox
dream
family
fish
kiss
lady
lake
class
box
bush
banjo

Page 152 boys
feet
buses
peaches
cars
children
dreams
flags
mixes
books
dishes
heroes

Page 153 teeth
lives
kisses
men
bosses
wishes
dogs
balls
tuna
beaches
puzzles
cakes
circuses
cats

Page 154 girl
prefix
lunch
man
wish
echo
cake
ball
mouse

Page 155 Carol slowly walked to the corner after soccer practice yesterday and waited for the bus. There were three other girls waiting and they were sitting on a bench. Carol was tired and asked if she could sit down, too. One of the girls stood up to give Carol her spot on the bench. Just then, the bus arrived, so Carol had to wait until she was on the bus before she finally sat down. She was so tired that she put her head back on the seat and fell fast asleep.

The second-graders were visiting a farm. The students saw horses and chickens. There were six cows and seven sheep. The students walked down the hill to a creek, where they saw frogs and fish. They went to the orchard, where they picked apples that were plump and juicy. The farmer showed them a pen where several calves were sleeping in the hay. The students got to pet some lambs, too. Then they climbed back on the bus for the long ride back to school.

Page 156 Ave.
Rd.
Ct.
Dr.
Ln.

19 Stinky Lane
14 Red Road
15 Pot Court
12 Bay Drive
16 Apple Avenue

Page 157 Mon.
Tues.
Wed.
Thurs.
Fri.
Sat.
Sun.

Thursday
Sunday
Friday
Monday
Wednesday
Saturday
Tuesday

Page 158 Jan. 1, 2012
Mar. 1, 2013
August 1, 2011
Sept. 1, 2012
December 1, 2013

Page 159   May
April
March
Dec.
Sept.
Oct.
Nov.
Jan.
July
June
Feb.

Page 160   My name is Susan Anne White. My initials are S. A. W.
His name is Tom Ulysses Black. His initials are T. U. B.
William David White is his name. His initials are W. D. W.
I am John Adam Smith. My initials are J. A. S.

Names will vary.

An initial is an abbreviation of a name.

Page 161
2. Will you meet me at the library?
3. The library is closed today.
4. We should open the door.
5. Should we open the door?
6. The puppy barked at me.
7. Are you sure this is the right book?
8. Who spilled the milk?
9. Where do you live?

Page 162   Sentences will vary.

Page 163
1. He lives at 123 Happy Place, Atlanta, Georgia.
2. Put the plates, bowls, cups, and napkins on the table.
3. Today is January 10, 2007.
4. I live at 456 Win Avenue, Weed, California.
5. Yesterday was January 9, 2011.
6. I went on vacation on Monday, July 9, 2008.
7. I'll get the hammer, saw, and nails.
8. I have a red ball, a blue ball, and a white ball.
9. The party was at 1010 Oak Street, Dallas, Texas.

Page 164
1. I need to study, so I'll go to my room.
2. Freddy likes spaghetti, but he doesn't like spinach.
3. Will you go to the party, or will you stay home?
4. I got really sleepy, so I went to bed.
5. I like to play the piano, but I don't play very well.
6. You can have pizza, or you can have a hamburger.

Page 165
2. He yelled, "Get out of here! The boat is sinking!"
3. I said, "She knows that we are late."
4. James asked, "Is it time to go to the dentist?"
5. Jacob said, "Go away. I am trying to sleep."
6. She said, "There are seven dogs in my yard."
7. Mary said, "Stop playing and come in for lunch."
8. "We're having hot dogs," she said.
9. "The red rose is the prettiest," Ellen said.

Page 166
1. Dad said, "Go to bed."
2. "I have a cold and feel rotten," Mike said.
3. "I want to eat my lunch early," she said.
4. "I won the game," she said.
5. "Wow! I made the honor roll," Bill said.
6. "I live at 6 Green St.," Nel said.
7. Kim said, "My favorite colors are red, green, and blue."
8. Janet said, "I am a good student at school."
9. "My name is Jim, and I am visiting," he said.

Page 167
10. Ian asked, "Is today Jan. 1, 2011?"
11. Ann said, "Our flag is red, white, and blue."
12. He shouted, "Throw me the ball!"
13. "Wow! James won the race," Emily yelled.
14. "Mike lives in Atlanta," Bob said.
15. J.T. said, "Math is my best subject."
16. "The test was hard," Jennifer said.
17. I said, "Mr. Jones is my teacher."
18. Megan asked, "Who was first?"
19. Tim said, "The game is cancelled."
20. "Let's go to the park," Gary said.
21. "I was born on May 1, 1997," Sue said.

Page 168
2. Brett said, "We won't leave for an hour."
3. "That kitten is cute," said Devon.
4. "He also has a dog," Jenny said.
5. "Go lie down and rest," said his mother.
6. "This fudge is good," said Mike.
7. Sam asked, "Did you eat it all?"
8. Jenna said, "I was born on May 13, 2000."

Page 169
"Rover ran away," James said.
His sister asked, "Are you sure?"
"Yes. I looked in the backyard, and he isn't there. He isn't in the garage, and he isn't in his doghouse," James said.
His sister asked, "Did you look in our house?"
"No," James said.
He went to the house and climbed the steps. He opened the front door. Then he turned to his sister and he had a big smile on his face.
"Rover is in the house," said James.

Page 170
1. "Wow!" yells Bobby.
2. Billy yelled, "Stop!"
3. "Yikes!" she shouted.
4. "Yes!" he exclaimed.
5. "Help!" she cried.
6. Jim shouted, "Wait!"
7. "Wait!" she shouted.
8. "No!" he exclaimed.
Sentences will vary.

Page 171
1. "Oh, wow!" he said.
2. He exclaimed, "There's an alligator in here!"
3. He cried, "Get me some bandages!"
4. "I'm scared!" she cried.
5. "I love it!" he exclaimed.
6. He exclaimed, "Get out of the way!"
7. He yelled, "We just won the lottery!"
8. "Stop!" she cried.
Sentences will vary.

Page 172
1. 1
2. 10
3. She doesn't see well. She wears thick glasses. 6
4. 3, 1, 5, 2, 4

Page 173 Paragraphs will vary.

Page 174
	a snake	a zebra
an ear	a telephone	an egg
a cow	an umbrella	an alligator
a bear	an ant	a pig

Page 175
an elephant	a fox	a feather
a skunk	an astronaut	a yo-yo
a cone	a cup	a football
a cake	a flower	an igloo

Page 176
a goat	a gorilla	a dog
a sheep	an airplane	an apple
an envelope	a key	a cat
an arm	a hat	a bike

Page 177
1. Sam hit a grand slam.
2. Sam caught a fly ball.
3. Sam made a homerun.
4. Sam made an error on first base.
5. Sam made an out.
6. Sam made a base hit.
7. Sam had a great game.
8. Sam had a pizza after the game

Page 178 Sentences will vary.

Page 179
1. He ate an apple.
2. He ate a sandwich.
3. He drank an orange soda.
4. He ate a hot dog.
5. He ate an egg.
6. He ate a candy bar.
7. He ate an ice cream cone.
8. He drank a glass of milk

Page 180 Sentences will vary.

Page 181
1. Each Easter, Eddie eats eighty Easter eggs.
2. Goats gathered and gorged on grain.
3. Twelve twins twirled and twinkled.
4. Sister Susie sat sewing seven suits.
5. Betty Botter bought some bitter butter.
6. The witches wore watches.
7. A big black bug bit a big black bear.

Page 182 Sentences will vary.

Page 183 Sentences will vary.

Page 184
1. I am a ring.
2. I am a ball.
3. I am a cake.
4. I am a bed.
5. I am a bat.

Page 185
plum
grape
cherry
peach

plum   grape   cherry   peach
Examples of rhyming words:
thumb, shape, hairy, speech

Page 186   1. cat and rat
2. bug
3. rat

	cat	dog	bug	rat
	Y	N	N	N
	N	Y	N	N
	N	N	N	Y
	N	N	Y	N

Page 187   1. black
2. yellow
3. red

	yellow	red	black	silver
Aki	N	Y	N	N
Jack	N	N	Y	N
Dad	Y	N	N	N
Mom	N	N	N	Y

Page 188   dog
cat
pig

dog   cat   pig
Examples
blog   bat   big

Page 189   You call me a bear.
You call me a seal.
You call me a frog.

bear   seal   frog
Examples
stair   meal   jog

Page 190   goat   turtle
mouse   snake
reindeer   crocodile
whale   bat

Page 191   eagle   giraffe
rabbit   raccoon
oyster   rat
               horse

Page 192   tiger   turkey
fish   dinosaur
cow   camel

Page 193   boat
ship
truck
bicycle
Examples
car, bus, subway, plane

Page 194   blue
yellow
orange
green
Examples
black, gray, brown, pink

Page 195   One day, a little girl walked deep into the forest. She got tired of walking and decided to rest under a tree. Just then, forty fat frogs came hopping through the woods.

"Where are you going?" the little girl asked the frogs.

"We are going to town," one of the frogs answered, "where we will wander with a dozen dirty dogs."

As soon as the frogs left, a horse happened by. When the little girl saw it, she cried, "Oh, won't you please give me a ride?"

The horse saw how tired the little girl was, so it agreed. The little girl climbed up on the horse and rode it home. And forever after that, the horse and the little girl were fast friends.

Page 196   2. The crowd will come to hear the band.
3. The ants were crawling on the picnic table.
4. I went to the zoo and saw a bear.
5. The house is over there.
6. The moon is over their house.
7. Those rays from the sun are warm.
8. Please pour me some milk.
9. My throat is sore.
10. Please bring me a pail of water.
11. I might want to go.
12. Please stay out of sight.

Page 197

pair   knight   night   pear

24
12
12
Middle tree should be circled.

Page 198 2. My cat's tail is white.
3. His son went home.
4. We had a pear for a snack.
5. I'll meet you after school.
6. The ship was lost at sea.
7. We had a pair of rabbits.
8. My mother went to a garage sale.
9. Bob told a tall tale.
10. The sun was very bright.

Page 199 11. That hour went by fast.
12. We had meat and vegetables for dinner.
13. We walked down the road.
14. The window pane is broken.
15. That knot was hard to untie.
16. He rode his bike to school.
17. Carl carried a pail of water.
18. Sue has a pain in her leg.
19. Mike has a sailboat.
20. We saw a bear at the zoo.
21. That color is too pale.
22. I do not want to go.
23. I see the birds in the nest.
24. My feet are bare.
25. We went down to the cellar.
26. John was the seller of the car.

Page 200 2. Mary ate all the cookies.
3. The deer ran across the road.
4. The bee stung me.
5. Here I am.
6. Tim made his bed.
7. My aunt visited us today.
8. The wind blew really hard.
9. He had a patch over one eye.
10. She knows the rules of the game.

Page 201 11. Sue's hair is red.
12. Her collar kept her neck warm.
13. The piece of gum cost one cent.
14. Mike will be there soon.
15. There were eight puppies.
16. The flower had a pretty scent.
17. Did you hear from your sister?
18. They have a maid to clean the bedrooms.
19. The ant followed the sugar trail.
20. A hare has longer ears than a rabbit.

21. He had a runny nose.
22. The sky is blue.
23. The caller wanted to talk to Jim.
24. You begin a letter with "dear."
25. We voted for Mike.
26. My brother is four years old.

Page 202 2. We need to buy Polish (or polish) sausage and shoe polish.
3. Is there a tear in your eye because of the tear in your shirt?
4. I am close to the door so I will close it.
5. Live animals live at the zoo.
6. My mom presents my presents to me on my birthday.

Page 203 2. The center black part of your pencil is lead.
3. A guide dog can lead a blind person.
4. The wind blew the door open.
5. Don't forget to wind the clock.
6. I will not desert my friends in the desert.
7. We cannot see germs because they are so minute.
8. Sixty seconds equals one minute.
9. She has a beautiful bow in her hair.
10. The dancers will bow to the audience.

Page 204 dove/dove
wind/wind
Sentences will vary.

Page 205 bow/bow
presents/presents
lead/lead
desert/desert
Sentences will vary.

Page 206 2. The cat is my favorite pet.
I like to sit and pet my cat.
3. The artist will paint another picture.
I accidentally sat in some wet paint.
4. My family will take a trip to the lake this summer.
If you don't watch where you're walking, you might trip.
5. My little brother likes to play with his blocks.
I went to see the play with my parents.
6. Please check to make sure we have enough milk.
My grandmother gave me a check for my birthday.

7. Please tell me your name and address.
I am going to name my dog Rufus.

Page 207
2. Make a wish and blow out the candles.
3. A triangle is a shape.
4. I'm going to take a walk through the park.
5. Green is my favorite color.
6. Dad bought a spare tire for the car.
Verb examples
2. He will wish for a football.
3. Try to shape the clay into an animal.
4. Will you please walk the dog?.
5. Libby will color the picture.
6. The kids tire me out.

Page 208
1. Joey and I are friends.
2. He and I are like brothers.
3. He likes to talk to me on the phone.
4. I like to talk to him on the phone.
5. He likes to play with me.
6. He and I like to play soccer.
7. Sometimes I like to go to his house.
8. Sometimes he wants to come to see me.
9. He and I both like to play soccer.
10. I like to read to him.
Sentences will vary.

Page 209
1. Joy and I are friends.
2. She and I are like sisters.
3. She likes to play with me.
4. She and I like to fish.
5. Sometimes I like to go to her house.
6. Sometimes she wants to come to see me.
7. She and I both like to read.
8. I like to read to her.
9. She likes to read to me.
10. She likes to call me on the phone.
Sentences will vary.

Page 210
Yesterday, the dogs were eating.
Yesterday, I was feeding the dogs.
Yesterday, the girl was feeding the dogs.
Yesterday, the girls were feeding the dogs.

Page 211
Yesterday, the cat was eating.
Yesterday, the cats were eating.
Yesterday, I was feeding the cat.
Yesterday, the boys were feeding the cats.

Page 212
Yesterday, the clowns were giving the children a balloon.
Yesterday, the clown was giving the girl a balloon.
Yesterday, the children were getting a balloon from the clown.
Yesterday, I was giving the girl a balloon.

Page 213
1. Yesterday was my birthday.
2. I was eight years old.
3. I was very happy.
4. My family was at my party.
5. My friends were there.
6. My grandmother was there.
7. My cousins were there.
8. My cake was chocolate.
9. My balloons were red.
10. It was a great day.
Sentences will vary.

Page 214
1. Yesterday was my first soccer game.
2. I was proud to be on the team.
3. I was very happy.
4. My family was at my game.
5. My friends were there.
6. My grandmother was there.
7. My cousins were there.
8. My uniform was red and white.
9. My hat was red.
10. It was a great day.
Sentences will vary.

Page 215
Some ants were running about in search of food. One ant came across a chrysalis that was very near its time of change. The chrysalis moved its tail and attracted the attention of the ant, who then saw that it was alive.

"Poor animal!" cried the ant. "How sad! While I can run around at my pleasure, you lie here with the power only to move a joint or two of your tail."

The chrysalis heard all this but did not try to make any reply. A few days later, when the ant was passing that way again, nothing but the cocoon remained. Wondering what had become of its contents, the ant felt himself suddenly shaded and fanned by the wings of a beautiful butterfly. The butterfly said, "Boast now of your powers to run and climb."

Then, the butterfly rose in the air and was soon lost to the sight of the ant forever.

Page 216 1. 2, 4
2. 6
3. They had picnics every day. 6, 8
4. 1, 4, 5, 2, 3

Page 217 Paragraphs will vary.

Page 218 fact
inference
fact
inference

Page 219 fact
inference
inference
fact

Page 220 inference
fact
fact
inference

Page 221 inference
fact
fact
inference

Page 222 2. Fact
3. Fact
4. Fact
5. Fact
6. Fact
7. Opinion
8. Fact
9. Opinion
10. Opinion

Page 223 Facts will vary.

Page 224 Opinions will vary.

Page 225 Sentences will vary.

Page 226 real
nonfiction
Sentences will vary.
not real
fiction
Sentences will vary.

Page 227 Stories will vary.

Page 228 Stories will vary.

Page 230 not real
fantasy
Example
He cast a spell with a wand.

Page 231 real
nonfiction

not real
fantasy
Example
The cow jumped over the moon.

Page 232 Stories will vary.

Page 233 nonfiction
nonfiction
nonfiction
fiction
nonfiction
fiction

Page 234 real
nonfiction

not real
fiction
Example
There is no magic.

Page 235 prose
Sentences will vary.

Page 236 prose
Sentences will vary.

Page 237 fly, why
verse
Sentences will vary.

Page 238 smell/well
nose/blows
2 and 4   6 and 8
Sentences will vary.

Page 239 1. yes
2. yes
3. no
4. no

Page 240 fable

Page 241 fable
fairy tale

Page 242 Cinderella
Jack and the Beanstalk
Snow White and the Seven Dwarves
The Princess and the Pea

Page 243 Little Red Riding Hood
The Three Little Pigs
The Tortoise and the Hare
Goldilocks and the Three Bears

Page 244   1. fable
2. a. Do unto others as you would have them do unto you.

Page 245   1. fable
2. b. Little by little does the trick.

Page 246   Folk tales and answers will vary.

Page 247   Pictures and answers will vary.

Page 248   The story took place on Saturday morning.
The story took place in a tree.

Page 249   The story took place on Saturday morning.
The story took place in Billy's backyard.

Page 250   2. messy

Page 251   Arthur is pushy.
Arthur would run to get in front of everyone.

Page 252   1. The conflict is between the boy and nature.

Page 253   2. The conflict is between the boy and himself.

Page 254   3. The conflict is between the boy and his sister.

Page 255   3. Spiders and insects
4. Differences between spiders and insects

Page 256   2. Butterflies
4. Butterflies are insects.

Page 257   2. Ladybugs
4. Ladybugs are insects.

Page 258   3. Honesty is its own reward.

Page 259   2. It isn't always easy to be brave.

Page 261   Alternative endings will vary.

Page 262   Problem: Rosie was afraid she'd oversleep and miss the bus.
Solution: She set her alarm clock.

Problem: Jason was just starting to eat a popsicle when his mother asked him to get the mail.
Solution: He put the popsicle back in the freezer so it would not melt.

Page 263   Problem: Mercedes had only one mitten.
Solution: Elena had three and gave one to Mercedes.
Stories, problems, and solutions will vary.

Page 264   2. trees
3. body parts
4. furniture
5. subjects
6. places to eat
7. dogs
8. countries

Page 265   1. parts of a paragraph
2. clothing
3. tools
4. relatives
5. measurements
6. shapes
7. face parts
8. months

Page 266   2. ~~freeze~~, ways to cook
3. ~~sandwich~~, liquids
4. ~~mountain~~, bodies of water
5. ~~finger~~, on your head
6. ~~sofa~~, window covers
7. ~~friend~~, relatives
8. ~~month~~, times of the day

Page 267   1. ~~duck~~, have four legs
2. ~~mouth~~, things that fasten
3. ~~fall~~, months
4. ~~cloud~~, bodies of water
5. ~~third~~, units of time
6. ~~January~~, days of the week
7. ~~comb~~, tools
8. ~~squash~~, fruit

Page 268
5 moose	2 moose
2 frog	5 frog
6 elephant	1 elephant
1 ant	6 ant
3 raccoon	4 raccoon
4 tiger	3 tiger

Page 269
5 sea	2 sea
3 pond	4 pond
6 ocean	1 ocean
1 drop	6 drop
4 lake	3 lake
2 puddle	5 puddle

Page 270
1 basketball	6 basketball
6 pea	1 pea
4 ping-pong ball	3 ping-pong ball
3 plum	4 plum
2 baseball	5 baseball
5 marble	2 marble

Page 271   2 cantaloupe   5 cantaloupe
3 grapefruit   4 grapefruit
4 orange   3 orange
6 cherry   1 cherry
1 watermelon   6 watermelon
5 plum   2 plum

Page 272   **Swim**   **Both**   **Fly**
bass   duck   bat
salmon   gull   crow
seal   goose   eagle
shark   swan   wren
walrus   raven
whale   robin

Page 273   **2 legs**   **4 legs**   **0 legs**
bird   cat   snake
chicken   squirrel   fish
goose   dog   worm
bear

Page 274   1. Tuesday
2. Friday
3. Sunday
4. Wednesday
5. Saturday
6. Sunday
7. Saturday

Page 275   1. February
2. March
3. July
4. August
5. November
6. December
7. May
8. June

Page 276   5   **Page 277**   4
2   1
1   6
7   2
6   7
4   3
3   5

Page 278   7
2
3
4
1
6
5
10
9
8

Page 279   Garrett dropped the player and it stopped working.

3. The first time the player was dropped on the floor.

Page 280   1. May opened a door that hit Mr. Cho.
2. Mr. Cho threw his hands out.

Page 281   1. The reason Susan was late for class was that she missed the bus.
2. Susan was late for class on account of missing the bus.
3. Susan was late for class due to missing the bus.
4. Since it was getting dark, he went home.
5. A broken streetlight led to an auto accident.
6. Jim stayed home because he was afraid to ride in a plane.
7. The power outage was caused by the storm.

Page 282   1. Trees were blown down.
2. Many buildings and cars were damaged.
3. Whole houses were lifted in the air.

Page 283   1. The picnic was cancelled as a result of the rain.
2. They had to stop when their gas finally ran out.
3. Our car ran out of gas, thus we had to stop.
4. Mother wasn't home yet, so we couldn't go outside to play.
5. It was getting dark, therefore we went home.
6. We went inside, then it started to rain.

Page 284   Example
Uncle George will help the stranger.

Page 285   Example
Gloria won't go on the ride.

Page 286   1. to make something beautiful

1. sweat

Page 287   2. said with anger

2. called off

Page 288   1. 4
2. 3
3. She got her sister, Katy, to help her.   10
4. 5, 2, 1, 4, 3

Page 289   Paragraphs will vary.

Page 290
1. w
2. o
3. n
4. d
5. e
6. r
7. f
8. u
9. l
wonderful

Page 291

Page 292

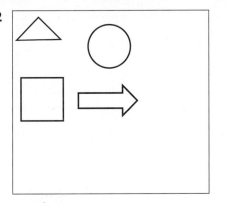

1. above
2. right
3. arrow

Page 293
1. Bird
2. right
3. Cat
4. left/Cat
6. right

Page 294
1. Bird/Dog
2. right/Dog Street
3. Dog Street
4. right/street

Page 295

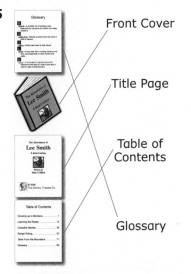

Front Cover

Title Page

Table of Contents

Glossary

Page 296
1. bedroll
2. lasso
3. jerky

Page 297
1. Campfire Stories
2. Growing up in Montana
3. Campfire Stories

Page 299
1. herring
2. hero, he's, hey
3. zoo
4. after
5. heron
6. hexagon
7. hero

Page 300

34 Summer Lane
Boise, ID 83401
August 1, 2010

Dear Sarah,
 I am having a great time at summer camp.

Sincerely,
Mike

Page 301

637 White Avenue
Seattle, Washington 98107
September 16, 2010

Dear Sam,
 I went to the park yesterday. I saw some white ducks in the pond.

Yours truly,
John

Page 302

3700 Pacific Avenue
Boise, Idaho 89401
October 30, 2010

Dear Mr. Jones,
 Thank you for reading my poem. I am glad you liked it.

Sincerely,
Lisa

Page 303

1700 Pacific Avenue
Boise, Idaho 89401
May 7, 2010

Dear Aunt Susan,
    Thank you for the hat. It will help me keep warm. You are sweet to remember my birthday.

Yours truly,
Lisa

———————————————

4327 Baker Avenue
Houston, Texas 77025
February 13, 2010

Dear Aunt Mary,
    Thank you for letting me stay with you. It was fun to play with your dogs.

Yours truly,
Eric

Page 304

1200 Brown Avenue
New York City, New York
May 7, 2010

Dear Mr. Smith,
    Thank you for the book. I like to read. You are kind to remember my birthday.

Yours truly,
Aaron

———————————————

Thank-you notes will vary.

1716 Circle Drive
Houston, Texas 77025
June 10, 2010

Dear Uncle Tom,
    I am having fun on my vacation. I went to the zoo yesterday.

Sincerely,
Mark

Page 305
1. Formal
2. Informal
3. Formal
4. Informal
5. Informal
6. Informal
7. Formal
8. Informal
9. Formal
10. Informal

Page 306   Letters will vary.

Page 308   E-mail letters will vary.

Page 309   address   return address   stamp

Judy Smith
64 Thomas Avenue
Atlanta, Georgia 30522

Jerald Black
46 Smith Street
Atlanta, Georgia 30522

Page 310   Judy Smith
64 Thomas Avenue
Atlanta, Georgia 30522

Jerald Black
46 Smith Street
Atlanta, Georgia 30522

———————————————

Ann Perry
32 Post Street
Seattle, Washington 98107

Robert White
6749 Ocean Avenue
Hanford, California 93230

Page 311   Maya Jones
45 Beacon Avenue
Dallas, Texas 40404

Simon George
63 Oak Street
Atlanta, Georgia 30522

———————————————

Jennifer Toledo
8 Pleasant Way
Hanford, California 93230

Angela Moyer
25 Concord Circle
Armona, California 93202

Page 312   Judy Smith
64 Thomas Avenue
Atlanta, Georgia 30522

Addresses will vary.

Page 313
1. gather & organize
2. draft
3. edit
4. revise

Page 314   Answers will vary.

Page 315 Drafts will vary.

Page 316 2
              1
              3
              4

Page 317   24 Olympic St.
                         Seattle, Washington 98107
                         May 3, 2010

              Dear Mary,
                  I am ~~hardly~~ not having a good
              time at my aunt's house. It has
              rained every day. Monday was the
              worst day. I will see you soon!

                         Yours truly,
                         Jennifer

Page 318 Short stories will vary.

Page 319 Short stories will vary.

Page 320 Short stories will vary.

Page 321 Short stories will vary.